STAGE CRAFTS

The kitchen scene from 'Fiddler on the Roof'. Other scenes from this production appear on pages 26 and 70.

STAGE CRAFTS

Second edition

Chris Hoggett

Heinemann
Portsmouth, NH

Fire precautions: see page 281 (under General Information) and also page 48.

This edition first published in the USA in 2001 by
Heinemann
A division of Reed Elsevier, Inc.
361 Hanover Street
Portsmouth, NH. 03801-3912
www.heinemanndrama.com

Offices and agents throughout the world

ISBN 0-325-00345-9

Second edition originally published in 2001 by
A & C Black (Publishers) Ltd.
35 Bedford Row
London WC1R 4JH

First published 1975

A CIP catalog record is available from the Library of Congress.

Printed and bound in Great Britain by The Bath Press

Contents

Each section has a detailed list of contents on the first page.

Acknowledgements

My grateful thanks are due to the following:

Photographs—Norman D. Sutherland, Cheltenham Camera Club, for giving many hours to photographing the various settings shown in the design section (pages 82 to 106) and on pages 116-120, 125-129, 136, 140, 143, 146, 153, 166, 188, 189, 191, 236 and 282; John Pilston for pages 105, 188 and 250; Rev. J. B. Abrami for pages 117, 121-123, 127, 144, 267 and 268 (right); Matthew Ruane for pages 84 (foot), 130 and 131; Patrick Gibson for page 104; Colin Willoughby for pages 244, 252, 256 and 263.

Permission to reproduce photographs—Professor John Holgate, Guildhall School of Music and Drama, for page 268 (foot); Cheltenham Newspaper Co. Ltd. for page 240.

The Rev. J. E. Maguire, O. Carm., headmaster of Whitefriars School, Cheltenham for his support and interest over many years of school productions; the Rev. B. Cunliffe, O. Carm., for lighting most of the productions shown in this book; the boys of the school for their assistance in making properties and scenery.

Peter and Sheila Mander for their helpful suggestions and criticism for the section on make-up; Peter Etheredge for his advice on painting and stage lighting.

My wife for her constant help and support throughout the preparation of the book.

I would also like to thank Rosemarie Swinfield for the additional material in the Make-up and Masks chapter (pages 244-63).

C. H. 2001

Introduction

This book is intended for all those who seek information on methods of design, construction and decoration for the stage. It is also intended as a source book in the various techniques of painting, printing and modelling suitable for the theatre.

The purpose throughout is to provide a practical visual approach – all constructional methods clearly seen with a minimum of text. Many techniques can be only lightly sketched in and it is hoped that those seeking further information will follow up the books listed in the reference section at the back of this book.

The layout of the book is straightforward: divided into eleven sections, it starts literally from ground level and develops gradually towards the final visual appearance of a production.

The sections

1 using an empty space, the construction of stage and superstructures, masking off the front, sides and back of the stage with curtains;

2 basic building units for independent stages, making rostra, steps, staircases and mobile units:

3 building the 'walls' of the stage: flats, their types and construction;

4 planning and design: the use of all the materials shown in sections 1–3, methods of planning, drawings, models and types of setting – ten examples:

5 decorating the set: painting of flats and cloths; printing and painting techniques;

6 furnishing the set: the design and manufacture of all 'properties' other than furniture;

7 lighting the set: types of lamp, equipment, arrangement of lights, lighting rehearsals;

8 arms and armour, dressing the characters;

9 costume accessories;

10 the final touches: make-up of characters;

11 glossary, index, list of suppliers, tools, materials, books, etc.

The acting area   1

STAGE BUILDING · CURTAINS · CLOTHS

THE ACTING AREA

The acting area may be an empty hall, a proscenium stage, a set of rostra or a set of curtains or screens – with or without staging. Sometimes a garden may be used for an outdoor production.

Whatever the area or space, check all dimensions carefully and all the facilities available round the space. Give thought to the possibility of experimenting with the area, keeping in mind the demands of the text and the director's concept of the play.

Certain essential questions should be answered before planning a production: will more than one level be needed for the movement of the play? Is the width of the hall or stage sufficient for storage of scenery and properties? Is there enough depth for a gangway behind the backcloth? Are the exits suitably placed?

Queries of this kind must be dealt with before the making of any preliminary sketches and plans.

These two pages show some of the solutions to filling and changing an acting area. The pages following deal with the various examples in more detail.

The empty space
(see page 6)

The empty space: consider it as an empty box enclosed by six sides – five planes consisting of floor, ceiling, three walls and an imaginary open side towards the audience.

Theatre-in-the-round: the empty space used as an acting area with seats encircling the space.

Arena space: seats raised on temporary rostra or platforms. (Arena seating is rarely permanent except in the Greek and Roman amphitheatres.)

Flexible wooden rostra, or metal frame and boards
(see pages 8–9)

The play may be staged on any level above the audience or be arranged on many levels. A stage that allows a wide variety of level and shape is that shown in **a** and **b**. (See pages 40–41 for the rostra staging units.)

If rostra or normal staging are not available, tubular steel or slotted angle framing can be used as a structure with duck-boarding to make the level.

Metal frame and boards

Superstructures
(see pages 12–13)

If the ceiling of a hall is unsuitable for fixing or hanging equipment and drapes, one can consider the possibility of a superstructure. Provided that there is sufficient height, a metal structure of angle or tubular steel can be built on or off the sides of the stage as a freestanding unit.

a *Twelve rostra units with three sets of steps.*

b *Rostra units arranged on two levels and with triangular apron and a ramp.*

Proscenium stage and aprons

(see pages 14–15)

Many halls already have a stage, often with a substantial proscenium opening and a complete set of drapes. Do not feel confined and unable to adapt this arrangement – rather consider the possibilities inherent in the apron front, a ramp down to the auditorium, steps and exits to the sides of the proscenium. Even the introduction of a new entrance/exit area may be considered if it helps the movement of players. Any idea should be considered if economically possible.

It may seem obvious to stage a play on an existing stage, but if the auditorium is large certain productions may be better suited to a central arena type of setting. Possibly a long gangway could be projected out from the stage with the audience arranged round it – rather like a fashion show! Always be prepared to experiment with the facilities at hand.

A permanent stage or a rostra stage built out to the full width of the hall (dotted lines indicate proscenium opening above).

As above, but with an apron fitted in front. The apron could be on a lower level.

As above, but with proscenium altered to accommodate side entrances and steps.

5

THE EMPTY SPACE

There are some basic considerations when planning an acting space for all types of production: the dimensions and facilities, the need to think of the hall or room as an empty space that will be used to full advantage for the particular production, and the practical problems involved.

Let us assume that there is an empty hall. Does the space available suggest, by its shape, size and, possibly, colour, a suitable acting area without making any fundamental alterations?

Two rows of benches arranged on three sides of the hall and a curtain against the fourth side would offer an acting area of extreme simplicity and economy. Where one or two rows of children could sit on the floor just in front of the benches, a considerable audience would be accommodated.

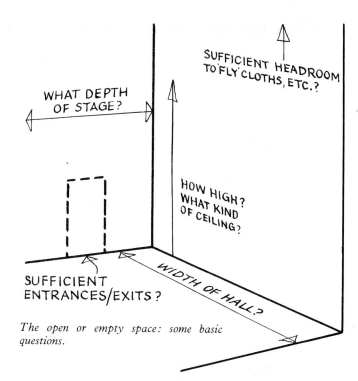

The open or empty space: some basic questions.

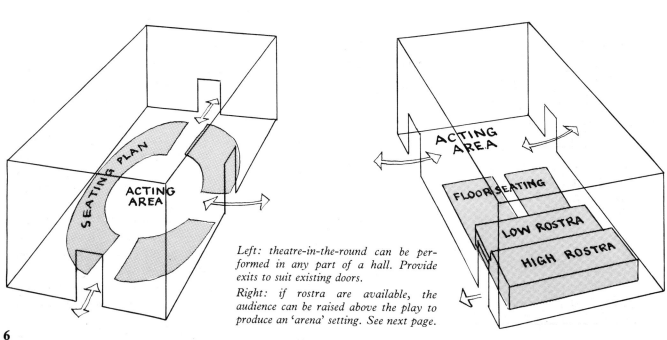

Left: theatre-in-the-round can be performed in any part of a hall. Provide exits to suit existing doors.

Right: if rostra are available, the audience can be raised above the play to produce an 'arena' setting. See next page.

Seating for theatre-in-the-round or 'arena' productions

slotted metal angle for rails

batten to retain chair legs

additional exit if required

18 SEATS BACK ROW

TWO ROWS OF 16 SEATS

15 SEATS

18 SEATS

19 SEATS

18 SEATS

19 SEATS

18 SEATS

GANGWAY

staggered seating

GANGWAY

ACTING AREA

‹ HIGH LEVEL ⋇ LOW LEVEL ›

ACTING AREA

Above: side elevation shows eye levels. If the ground-level seating is staggered, there will be better visibility.

With flexible rostra staging it is easy to adapt to all types of production. Here the usual role of the rostrum has been reversed – the audience replacing the actors.

The rails round the raised seating are essential for safety and to meet existing fire regulations – see note on page 281.

With sufficient rostra two sides can be built up to make a semi-arena setting.

Left: plan view of rostra layout. Two lines of higher rostra at the back, one line of lower rostra at the front.

FLEXIBLE WOODEN ROSTRA

With approximately 12 rostra (in proportions 6×4×3) and 4 rostra (6×4×1½) a great variety of shapes can be erected – note the three variations on the next page. If the building has an existing narrow stage, a large apron may be built with the rostra if the heights relate (small adjustments can be made by placing blocks beneath the rostra to increase the height).

'Horseshoe' layout – entrance through side door and centre gangway.

Using a corner of the hall.

Theatre-in-the-round.

Fascia boards

Rostra staging can be covered in front by fascia boards. Make them from 9 mm plywood cut to fit two, three or more rostra. Alternatives to plywood are hardboard or pinboard.

a 12 x 3 plywood fascia to cover three rostra

glued and screwed

9 mm. plywood

turn. keys

REAR SIDE

equals thickness of rostra leg

METAL FRAME AND BOARDS

If a permanent stage or rostra unit system is not available, a quick and practical stage can be assembled from a metal frame structure with duck-boards to cover the top. Tubular scaffolding and duck-boards can be hired from most large building contractors or suppliers. If scaffolding is not available, slotted metal angle (such as Dexion in U.K.) is an excellent alternative. Again, if duck-boards are difficult to obtain large sheets of composition chipboard (such as Weyroc in U.K.) or block-board are good substitutes provided that they are secured and strengthened on the underside with wood or metal strips – see the inset illustration.

The noise problem of actors' movements on boards that rest on a metal frame can be alleviated by covering with tarpaulin (also obtainable on hire or loan from some builders). Old canvas and underfelt are another useful sound-proofing. The footwear of the actors can also decrease the noise.

The amount of framing and boarding needed will depend on the space available and on the needs of the production.

Above: elevation showing duck-boards resting on metal frame. Allow clearance between the top of frame uprights and the underside of the boards.

joint pin used for connecting tubes end to end

TARPAULIN (Stage cloth)

DUCK BOARD

coupler for connecting tubing... ...at right-angles

base plate or rubber feet to protect the floor

swivel coupler connects tubes at any angle

BALCONY LEVEL BOARD

WOOD ROSTRUM

blade

connecting pocket

adjustable base plate for uneven surfaces

Above: angle-lock scaffolding – a variation on the traditional type shown opposite. Although more expensive to hire, it has the advantage of easy, quick erection.

Below: slotted angle frame with boards. Heavy-duty or medium frame are both suitable for staging.

wood strip to height of bolt heads gives level surface for boards – fix with screws and washers

wood batten fixed under stops movement of board

corner plate

SLOTTED ANGLE

BOARD

TARPAULIN CANVAS OR BLANKETS

FASCIA

turn-key

SUPERSTRUCTURES

Right: a cross-section through ceiling showing the lifting mechanism for a suspended superstructure. By lowering the structure to floor level, borders, wings, lighting and the structure itself are easily assembled and dismantled.

4 pulleys
joists
to winch
cable
board to bolt winch down
prepared ceiling holes
'U' bolt
2 50kg winches each taking 2 cables
superstructure

A *suspension method.*

B *front suspension with rear wall brackets.*

side projections if required

C *pillar supports.*

D *front pillars, rear brackets.*

A simple grid system can be built up with the metal angle. Most suitable is the Dexion (heavy duty) slotted angle which will carry tracks and battens for curtains, borders, wings, lighting and, if required, a proscenium arch.

Type '**A**' is suitable for a high ceiling with substantial timber beams or girder construction.

Frame construction

'U' bolt for cable

assembled framework

projections from sides if required

locking pin

welded 'eyes' for joining sections

If welding equipment is available, frame can be made of 3·8 cm barrel (tubular metal).

Tracks and battens

Tracks for traverse curtains, or piping and timber for battens may be attached to the basic structure in a number of ways:

simple clip suitable for supporting lighting battens

wing-nut fixture for easy assembly

'home-made' clip shaped from light alloy.

Assorted suspension clips and brackets for barrel.

frame attached to rear of proscenium

REAR OF PROSCENIUM

wood strip to secure curtain

curtain border

Fixing of borders, cut-outs or curtains can be to battens of slotted angle or wood.

A proscenium arch can be attached to the front projection of a superstructure.

PROSCENIUM STAGE

If a proscenium arch is needed over a temporary rostra stage, a simple structure of four flats with 50×25 mm wooden joining pieces can be erected. See pages 48–49 for construction of plain flats.

If the hall is very high, an additional pair of flats can be attached above the two horizontal flats (see dotted lines in the diagram below).

Above: an alternative to wooden framework is the barrel (tubular metal) or metal slotted angle.

gaps to top or sides (if any) can be filled by fixing stiff card or board to edge of flats

chain or cord supports can be effective for temporary fixtures

75×25 mm wood brace and joining strip

curtain track to suit weight of curtain material

a narrow reveal to give depth to proscenium arch – use narrow flats or planks of 30 cm wood

BRACE

SCREW EYE

BRACKET

assorted fixtures – the type dependant on wall and floor surfaces

Above: the assembled proscenium arch. If the hall is narrow, one horizontal flat may be enough. The pelmet board needs to be firmly braced; supporting flats will have to be attached to the rear side.

Curtain tracks are explained in the section on curtains and cloths.

ceiling of hall of tiles, plaster or wood? What type of fixing ensures maximum safety and protection?

if flats touch ceiling a line of felt along top edge will protect ceiling and remove any gaps

additional flats at top give extra height if required

plywood joining plate

pelmet for proscenium curtains should over hang reveals to allow curtains to open fully

braces of 75 x 25 mm. wood, metal slotted angle or chain and cord.

curtain tracks

WIDE DOOR FLAT

50 x 50 mm. wood brace or metal angle to hold proscenium sides.

FASCIA TO PELMET

hardboard

heavy weights if screwing down will damage floor surface

APRON

reveal – 30 cm flat

continuous cord for sets of curtains (see page 20)

A more elaborate temporary proscenium consisting of two wide-door flats with rounded arches. Each arch has an independent curtain track system.

The four horizontal flats may be reduced to two if larger flats are available, or a special flat can be constructed – see the section on flats.

POSITIONING OF CLOTHS, BORDERS & WINGS

Masking a stage, whether permanent or erected for the occasion, requires careful planning. The backcloth, borders and wings must be placed in relation to the proscenium edges. Before considering the borders, the background cloth or curtain should be positioned approximately one metre from the back wall to allow a free passageway behind.

Borders should hang about level with the top of the proscenium arch. Note that the height of wing flats is level with the tops of borders – see page 47 for construction of flats.

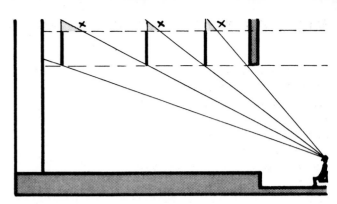

The deeper the stage the more borders will be needed. (Note how the spacing widens towards the backcloth.)

Incorrect positioning: the shaded area, called the 'non-masking triangle', is wasteful of material and may not mask the lighting battens.

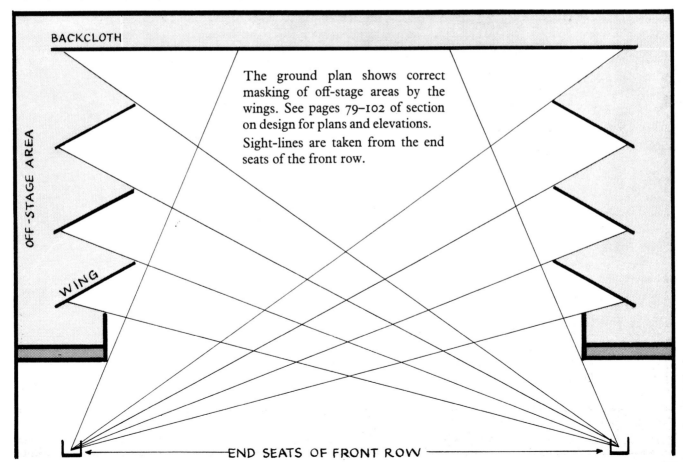

BACKCLOTH

OFF-STAGE AREA

WING

The ground plan shows correct masking of off-stage areas by the wings. See pages 79–102 of section on design for plans and elevations.

Sight-lines are taken from the end seats of the front row.

END SEATS OF FRONT ROW

Labels in illustration: back traverse tabs · 3rd border · 1st border · front cloth (rolled up) · 2nd border · PROSCENIUM ARCH · backcloth (partly lifted) · proscenium border · AUDITORIUM · 3rd wing · 2nd wing · 1st wing · proscenium traverse tabs · back curtain · DOWN STAGE LEFT

CURTAINS AND CLOTHS

Most schools, halls, church-halls and other similar buildings are fitted out with a 'curtain set', consisting of wings, back-curtain (and/or backcloth) and borders.

Frequently, in the space between a pair of wings and related border hangs a pair of traverse tabs (curtains that can be drawn across the stage to reveal or conceal the scene behind). Sometimes a painted backcloth or cloths will be used in conjunction with the curtain wings: the traverse tabs then come into use for changes of backcloth. The proscenium curtain is usually made of a pair of traverse tabs.

Traverse tabs for proscenium opening and elsewhere.

iron brackets

steel, iron or plastic rod

PROSCENIUM

75 × 25 mm supporting wood.

This pair can be drawn by hand – a track system is described on following pages.

small hooks can be used for light-weight materials

Borders can be fitted by using a track system.

track

border

swivel bolt or wing-nut and bolt

Wing curtain.

wide angle of movement

or large screw-eyes

Small curtains can be hung on a metal bracket attached to a post or on the edge of a flat.

support
runners
double track
curtain here

Cross-section of track for heavy-duty curtains.

A diagrammatic view of pulley system and fixing of tabs 'x' to the continuous cord.

300 mm X 25 mm PELMET BOARD

Proscenium curtains

A pair of traverse tabs can be operated by using a continuous cord fixed over four pulleys.

The low pulley should be firmly attached to the floor – a tension spring fitted between the low pulley and the floor will help to keep the cord taut.

A windlass (see above) may replace the hand-pulling method.

Diagrammatic view of pulleys and fixing sets of ties 'x' to the cords.

1 way   2 way   single double

Some types of pulleys and cleats.

The winch. Useful for raising and lowering heavy curtains, cloths and superstructures (see page 12).

Alternative curtains

With this type of curtains, the two cords are pulled simultaneously and tied over cleats. Some theatres use small hand windlasses for the same operation.

The traverse style is often preferred.

21

lightly tack curtain to lintel

approx 1 metre from curtain to back wall

LINTEL

wood block to protect floor

A quick assembly of backcloth or curtain

If a performance is to take place in unfamiliar surroundings, a useful method of hanging back-curtains is to wedge them against the ceiling, as shown.

A preliminary survey and note of dimensions is needed and then the lengths of timber cut as shown.

75 X 25 mm for 'lintel'

hinge or notch to secure post

cut three lengths of 75 X 25 mm timber to height of hall

tighten posts by pulling towards curtain sides

wood block slide

Arrangement of supports.

Rolling up a backcloth

A backcloth may be hired or purchased from the appropriate supplier – see page 276. If it is desired to 'fly' the cloth, assemble as shown. Use two pieces of 50 × 25 mm timber to 'sandwich' the cloth and tapes at the top edge, securing with screws. A cylinder attached to the cloth may be hired or made from a long wooden pole or metal tube. Metal will be suitable only if of a light alloy such as aluminium that can be drilled and attached to the lower edge of the cloth.

Pulleys should be arranged as shown, spaced out to fit the width of the cloth. See previous page but one for types of pulley.

curtain border

MAIN BATTEN

2-way pulley

2-way pulley

tapes (or cord) from cloth to main batten

sandwich battens (webbing along top edge as alternative)

second scene on backcloth No 2

CYCLORAMA

1-way pulley

curtain wings

line

double cleat on side wall

rope guide

BACKCLOTH No.1

cardboard, wood or metal roller or cylinder (usually in sections)

BACKCLOTH No.2

2

Gauzes and cut-cloths

Gauzes are thin, semi-transparent cloths used to achieve effects of illusion and surprise. They are frequently used in transformation scenes and where atmospheric effects of mist or fog are required. The more gauzes used, the more realism is achieved in the mist scenes. The whole quality of surprise and illusion is dependent on the correct placing of lights – which will be fully discussed in the section on lighting.

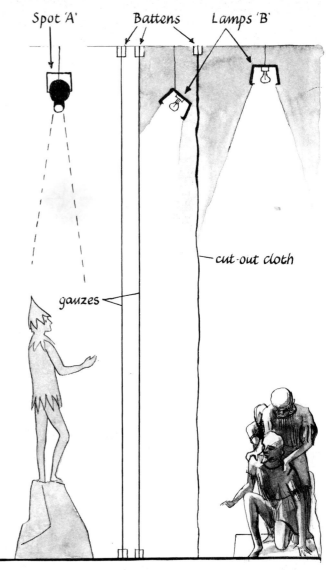

*Side elevation of the scene on the right: the standing figure is soon to appear before the figures crouching. This will occur the moment that spot **A** is lit – if the **B** lights are dimmed or cut off, the intensity of the effect will be increased.*

Cut-cloths are used for decorative effects. Pieces of gauze are for strengthening the more complex cut-out shapes. If the cut-out is very intricate, it is advisable to glue gauze to the back of the complete surface area. In the scene on the right, the cut-out shape of arching branches is achieved by this means.

cut-out cloth

bottom of
gauze

ground row
with ramp

ground row

rock 'props'

rock 'props'

The dotted figure will appear only when spot **A** *is on. The silhouette is achieved by lighting the gauze curtains immediately in the front. All other lamps are off. The effect of this kind of lighting technique on a painted gauze is illustrated on page* 127.

Fixing a temporary cyclorama

The skycloth or cyclorama should fill the back wall of the hall and can be easily assembled as shown. Build the framework of metal slotted angle to the height of the hall, allowing approximately 30 mm for inserting wedges. Further bracing can be added where appropriate. Ensure that the cloth is taped at top and sides and attached to the frame as shown. A barrel (tubular metal) is inserted in the pocket to pull the cloth taut.

A street scene from 'Fiddler on the Roof'. The silhouette effect is achieved by batten lighting on a temporary cyclorama as illustrated at the top of the page. The house construction is shown on page 46. The setting was built in a school hall by 15 and 16 year old boys as part of a craft course. Other scenes from the production are shown on pages 70 and 282.

Rostra

2

CONSTRUCTION · RAMPS · STEPS · TRUCKS

ROSTRA

Rostra, considered as building units for all kinds of stage-building, are most versatile pieces of equipment. As rectangular boxes they can be built into stages or can make new levels on an existing stage. In the form of ramps or steps they allow movement from one level to another and, with wheels or castor runners, they are the basis of mobile set pieces – useful for quick scene changes.

Rigid, non-collapsible rostra are also suitable for staging but are difficult to store away unless a large amount of storage space is available. One useful purpose for a rigid rostrum could be that of a wardrobe – ideal where space for clothing is inadequate – see drawing.

The construction of the basic unit shown here is of a collapsible type for convenience of storage. Variations of shape and size are shown in this section. They include the ramp, triangular and semi-circular rostra, steps and staircases, and spiral and curving assemblies.

An example of a basic rostra stage with a ramp and five individual step units making a four-level set is shown on pages 40–41. It is also featured in the section on design as the arrangement used for a production of 'The Merchant of Venice' (see pages 92–93).

rostrum top 18 mm. plywood

screwed and glued battens 50x25mm to prevent movement

centre board (position here)

closed position for storage

Collapsible rostra–1

Drawings and plans on these pages show the construction of a large rostrum measuring $6 \times 4 \times 3$. Whatever the size, a top board of 18 mm plywood and a 12 mm centre-board will be necessary. Chip- or blockboard may be substituted for the centre-board if more convenient.

A number of such rostra will be suitable for building an independent stage. (The height of 3 units is always optional – some people may prefer a lower level.)

This type of rostra is seen in the stage assembly on page 99.

Side elevation of rostrum.

100 X 50 mm. softwood frame

6 UNITS

4 UNITS

C

plywood or composition board

25 X 25 mm slides

Plan view of rostrum.

rostrum for stage and/or wardrobe
plywood top and sides
rostrum top and back of wardrobe
rail
flush fitting lock
bolts
rigid framework

Wardrobe: the frame must be of a fixed type or be braced at the back to keep it rigid. Sides and top can, as required, be covered with thin plywood or hardboard. Doors are added at the front.

Mortice and tenon joint as at **A**.

Halving joint as at **B**.

Slides for centre-board as at **C**.

29

Collapsible rostra–2

Smaller rostra can be constructed more simply. A rostrum measuring approximately 1.5 m × 1 m, as illustrated here, does not require a centre-board and the top can be built of planking.

The hinging arrangement is also simpler but in the folded position the rostrum takes up rather more linear space when stored.

wide batten

18 mm thick planks (or board)

hinge position

folded position

A more elaborate hinging method gives a true right-angle to the frame when it is opened out, and closes up all the corners.

The sides of all the rostra shown may be faced with thin plywood or hardboard if they are to be used individually. If the rostra are used as a large group (e.g. for staging) only the visible faces need be covered.

set hinge into frame

A

hinge positions

B

x

x

A

B

ground plan showing closing movement

Ramps

100 × 38 mm softwood frame

18mm planks or plywood

CENTRE BOARD

glued wood blocks to fix centre board

battens to fit sockets

Smaller ramps will not require a centre-board or notches.

The sides may be covered with plywood or hardboard.

200 × 25 mm softwood or board

3mm plywood or hardboard

An interesting and dramatic way of moving from one level to another is by means of ramps. The construction and joints are similar to those of 'box' rostra apart from the join at the lower edge. These are rigid frame rostra not suitable for folding.

Triangles and curves

Triangular rostrum: hinging is similar to that shown on page 29.

ROSTRA TOP

screw down top to make permanent structure

18 mm plywood, board or plank

glued & tacked 3mm. plywood

wood blocks to make up curve

glued right-angled wood blocks

Semi-circular rostrum: this is also a rigid framework. It could be built as two quarter circles for convenience of carrying and storage.

remove existing pin from hinge and insert a nail – remove for storage

to close

columns of two (or more) rostra

3mm plywood tacked & glued to wood frame – see page 145 on making columns

Cylindrical rostra are useful for seating on stage. A group can be assembled to make columns.

Steps – 1

Steps from auditorium to stage need to be wide – approximately 2 metres or more. They will then accommodate large casts for exits and entrances through the auditorium; they will also provide useful space for standing and sitting at different levels.

The steps shown are in three parts: the one at the base is 1 × 2 metres, the one in the middle 66 cm × 2 metres and the one at the top 33 cm × 2 metres. Placed against the front of the stage or apron, these rostra provide four steps, each being one quarter of the height of the stage or apron.

16 mm. plank
3 mm plywood
wood blocks glued and screwed

height of stage

small wooden blocks to prevent movement

¼ height of stage

Adaptable set of steps and rostrum

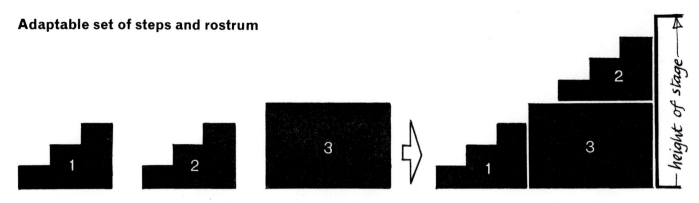

Two sets of treads and one small rostrum: the riser is 20 cm, the tread 30 cm, the rostrum 80 cm high × 120 × 120. This arrangement gives 8 steps if the last step on to the stage is included.

Some variations with the same equipment: variations 3, 4 and 5 will require an additional rostrum.

large rostra or stage level

Steps – 2: Staircases

This flight of steps is built in two sections, each constructed over a well-braced framework.

metal frame balcony

300 mm x 18 mm. treads of softwood, board or plywood

225 mm x 9 mm risers

top of flight 'A'

19 mm. board or plywood

'EXPLODED' PART VIEW OF FLIGHT 'B'

bracing can be glued and screwed or jointed

FLIGHT 'B'

FLIGHT 'A'

face sides with canvas

mortice and tenon

Staircase with a landing

When more complex stair arrangements are required and a landing or balcony is to be the focal point of the scene, a construction similar to this may be attempted.

metal frame balcony level

fascia

balcony height equals seven steps

triangular rostrum

fascia here

BALCONY

UP

UP

UP

construction of steps as shown on page 34

This group of stairs shows two directions down from a balcony. The central triangular rostrum serves as a resting point and a possible change of direction. The smaller steps have solid sides of composition board. The risers are not weight-bearing and can be made from hardboard.

Photographs on pages 96–99 show one way of using this type of staircase in a setting.

Steps – 3:
Spirals and curves

wall or rails as appropriate on outer edges

top

centre post to height of top level

middle

lower

outer edges project here if only 3 supporting sides are built — (6 sides will result in flush finish)

balcony level

butt joints

30°

50x50mm bracing frame

screw or cramp sections together

18 mm blockboard or plywood (broken lines)

Spirals are best constructed in smaller units of two or three steps. Divide the turn by the number of degrees to each step. In this example, there are 30°.

top section

middle section

lower section

felt covering

blockboard or plywood treads

18 mm plywood

UNIT 'A'

50×50 mm bracing

Curved staircases are a pleasing variation from the angular units. They can be constructed in concave (**A**) or convex (**B**) curves.

curved unit

STEP

80°

STEP

UNIT 'B'

exploded view of unit 'B'

step treads of blockboard or plywood

3 mm plywood or hardboard risers

18 mm. plywood or blockboard

50×50 mm bracing

Curved unit **A** above can be linked into other sets of straight steps as shown here. The amount of turn is dependent on the shape of the scene. Here there is a turn of approximately 80°.

STEPS ROSTRUM STEPS

UNIT B

The convex unit **B** is designed to fit against an apron or wall but can also be linked to steps on one or both sides. This would make an interesting end to a 'thrust' or projecting stage.

39

UNIT E

UNIT B

height of this unit equal with triangular rostrum

UNIT D

UNIT A

UNIT C

rostra treads & top – 18 mm board or 300×25 mm plank

3 mm plywood or hardboard for risers

50×50 mm legs 50×25 mm horizontals

A basic 4-level rostra system

This page shows the five units that together make the staging on four levels shown opposite. The 'ground' (or main stage) level is built of rostra and includes a ramp and step to make an entrance from the side of the auditorium.

Alternatively the five-unit assembly can be placed on an existing stage with an apron extension, or on the floor of a hall with simple curtain or screen backings.

The arrangement shown opposite was used for a production of 'The Merchant of Venice' described in the section on design (see pages 92–93).

Trucks – 1

allow 15 mm from bottom of truck to floor level

Trucks (in effect rostra on wheels) are highly adaptable scenic devices, allowing quick changes of scene. They can be run on rails, as shown below, be independent on castors, as illustrated opposite, or be revolved on a hinge as shown on the ground plan and photographs on pages 103 and 106.

ROSTRUM TOP

cardboard cylinders for logs

A truck based on the wheelbarrow principle. Two wheel or ball castors fixed to the rear of the truck with two hand grips at the front. Lift to push into position, lower to achieve stability. Illustrated on page 70.

part of moveable scene on 'A' truck

fixed scene

slide of truck 25×25 mm

3 mm base for rails

double rail for sliding small trucks without wheels – wax bottom with candle

castor

25 × 25 mm 'railway' nailed to stage.

TRUCK A

TRUCK B

fixed set piece

proscenium

Two trucks – or more if required – can be used in conjunction with a set piece, allowing a wide range of quick scene changes.

truck unit A

truck unit B

castors

bracing behind stove

PLAN OF UNIT 'A'

castors

bracing behind fire

PLAN OF UNIT 'B'

BACK UNIT A

BACK UNIT B

Two free-moving units

The two fireplaces shown above reveal, when reversed, either a long high wall or two smaller walls. Alternatively, another scene could be built and painted on the reverse sides. The fireplaces are made with thin plywood or hardboard on a 50×25 mm timber frame. See page 131 for an illustration showing 'wall' sides.

Castors   Various kinds of castor are available:

rubber tyre on spigot

swivel ball on spigot

swivel ball on flange

Small and medium-sized castors for revolving flats.

rubber tyre on spigot designed for tubular scaffolding

locking device

flange

rubber tyre on flange

Heavy-duty castors, suitable for trucks and large mobiles.

43

Trucks – 2: Revolving, free-turning

Sketch designs for a revolving truck

These small 'thumb-nail' sketches may serve as one method of thinking out an idea for scenic and constructional devices. A cardboard scale model should then be prepared to test the theory.

The example shown on these pages is based on a production of 'Romeo and Juliet' – see also the section on painting (page 129) for a method of treating the wall side of this mobile rostrum.

A small house for 'Fiddler on the Roof'. These small sketches illustrate ideas for the numerous scenes demanded by the text. The construction of this large revolving truck is shown on page 46. Photographs on pages 26, 70 and 282.

halving joints

hardboard facing on both sides (or canvas)

BED/TOMB

materials as box below

wood frame 50 x 25 mm

window

metal slotted angle for sub-structure and up three corners

'B'

'A'

floor covering of 18 mm plywood or blockboard, etc.

'C'

stage level

sub-structure

3 metres

wooden framework above of 50 x 25 mm. softwood

butt or halving joints

framing 50 x 25 mm softwood

covering of 3 mm plywood or hardboard

BENCH/BED

wood block to equal other angle

AN ALTERNATIVE SUB-STRUCTURE USING SCAFFOLDING

rubber castors (see p. 43)

Construction of revolving truck - 1

This independent truck has as base an equilateral triangle. It offers a wall face and two interior settings suitable as backings to the acting area or as parts of a larger setting.

As it is very heavy, this mobile unit stands on the floor of a hall behind an area of rostrum staging, at a distance of about 1½ metres from the rear wall. The sub-structure could be removed if there were no rostrum staging between the audience and the truck. The three scenes can be used as required, possibly with flats or wing curtains.

Home-made turntables

Use can be found for this type of device where a dramatist demands many changes of scene. Turntables carrying three scenes allow one to face the audience while the others are being changed. The sides could fit into a gap formed by flats or curtains.

Alternatively, the sides can be left unmasked and two-part scenes shown by pointing a corner towards the audience.

walls of house~six canvas flats, two for large swing flat doors - 75×25 mm frames.

chimney position-sides of 3mm material on 50×25 mm frame

roof of canvas

75×25 mm frame for roof.

halving joints

100×25 mm roof and beam supports

beams built up with 3mm material for sides and 100×12 mm for the visible ends attached to beam supports by nails

three hinges to each swing door

dresser screwed to rails of flat

window frame - 25×25mm softwood all halving joints

shutters - 3mm material on 50×25mm frame

fireplace - all 3mm material, 18mm board to carry utensils

simulated fire in hearth 6 volt battery

fireplace 'bed' section - top in 18mm board 3mm sides

medium gauge metal slotted angle framework

closed position of swing doors

hasp & staple to link doors

3 large load-bearing castors - 10mm clearance between frame and floor.

3·6 metres wide

8 small stabilising ball castors

house door built within swing door framework

metal sill

ball castors on swing doors

Construction of revolving trucks – 2

This truck is larger than the one shown on the previous page. It offers four settings: two interiors and two exteriors. Note the heavy-duty castors and the smaller stabilizing castors along the sides of the slotted angle framework.

Flats

3

CONSTRUCTION · GROUND ROWS AND CUT-OUTS · DOORS · WINDOWS · SCREENS

FLATS

Stage scenery has traditionally been constructed from flats of varying shape and size. Their main function is to mask off the immediate back and sides of the stage, creating with the aid of paint and texture a new environment of mood and time. Although in some cases superseded by new materials and techniques, flats are – with curtains – still the most practical and versatile way of building height and width on the stage.

Flats consist of a wooden frame over which canvas is tightly stretched and tacked. The size of the frame is determined by hall ceilings and proscenium openings. The top of the frame should be level with the top of the borders in a proscenium theatre; this will be approximately 1 metre higher than the top of the proscenium arch – see lower illustration on page 16.

A wide selection of widths is desirable on a large stage for box sets (see pages 88–91) but for simple 'border and wing with curtains' a uniform width of about 1 metre is sufficient provided that the flats are correctly placed to mask the 'offstage' area (see page 17). For such a purpose, six wing flats will usually be enough, three for each side.

Canvas can be expensive. Hardboard can be substituted; it needs to be well glued and tacked and does, of course, add considerably to the total weight.

Variations on the basic unit and methods of securing flats to the stage are described on the following pages. The last few pages of this section deal with alternatives to cloths (screens and folding flats).

It is worth experimenting with a variety of materials on the surface of the basic unit: expanded polystrene, rag, torn and crumpled newspaper, plaster, etc. in order to achieve the required effect – see also the section on painting.

Canvas purchased from scenic suppliers is always fireproofed. If expanded polystyrene is used, it must be covered with a layer of muslin and then lightly plastered.

cleat

BRACE

RAIL

A   D

toggle

TOGGLE RAIL

STILE

CANVAS COVERED

B   C

throw line for cleating

The joints

Mortice and tenon

This is the strongest and most useful of the joints. The mortice should be cut into the rails, the tenon into stiles.

The hidden mortice should be used at bottom corners B and C for strength. The open mortice can be used at A and D for convenience.

Hidden mortice

peg

Open mortice

peg and/or screws →

Halving or cheek joint

This is easier than a mortice and tenon joint but less strong. It is suitable for a smaller frame.

corrugated fasteners

Butt joint

This is the simplest joint, made by fixing rail to stile with corrugated fasteners and a triangular plywood plate that is glued and nailed over the corner.

The halving and butt joints are quite adequate for most small frames, are quickly built and will withstand considerable use throughout a number of productions.

TYPES OF FLAT

| Plain | Door | Window | Fireplace |

Flats can be divided into two main groups: those that are rectangular and are used chiefly for interiors or simple functional sets and those that have at least one irregular edge – sometimes two or three – and are used chiefly for exteriors. The latter are called 'cut-outs' and are illustrated on the opposite page.

Basic room flats are shown above with variations for door, window and fireplace. The door flat can be used for window and fireplace as well by placing part **A** in different positions.

Other rectangular flats are sometimes hinged together and are then called 'book flats'. More than two hinged together make a screen.

50

Book flat

Screen – two 'books' joined – canvas-covered

ARCHITECTURAL FEATURE

A plywood profile attached before flat is covered with canvas or hardboard.

Original width of flat.

V

VOID

← webbing

alternative – a two-way hinge

Cut-outs

Cut-outs, both architectural and natural irregular shapes, sometimes require flats to be adapted for the purpose. In the tree form on the left a tall narrow flat is used. For the classical style window on the right a special frame is made to which a plywood or hardboard profile is glued.

halving or butt joints for joining cutout to original flat

VOID   VOID

Stretching the canvas

Scenic canvas, of flax or cotton duck, is purchased already fire-proofed in 36″ and 72″ widths (or their centimetre equivalents). Hessian is cheaper but does not last as long.

Inset 1.

canvas

the shoulder on canvas-pliers acts as a lever on edge of frame

1 Cut your canvas 2 cm longer than your flat frame then, working from the centre of one end, tack towards the corners. The line of tacks should be about 5 cm from the outer edge of the frame. (This will give sufficient area of canvas for glueing.)

always tack from centres towards corners

2 With a pair of pliers (preferably canvas pliers as shown) stretch canvas over the frame at the other end (see inset 1) while tacks are being inserted.

Glueing and trimming

A small cut at the corners will help the canvas to lie well and will prevent creasing.

Inset 2.

A book unit (2 flats hinged together) has an extra canvas strip glued over the join to conceal the hinges and the gap.

5 Complete the operation by trimming the canvas with a sharp knife approximately 3 mm in from the edge.

4 Press the canvas over the glued frame with a warm damp cloth, working out towards the edges. (See inset **2** for corners.)

3 When tacking is complete, turn back the canvas and glue the frame. The more foam that is worked up with the brush while glueing the better the adhesion.

TACKS

Joining and bracing flats

attach line through hole in stile with knot

single cleat

throw line

double cleat

sill

approx. position of backing flat

a commercial extending brace & weight

A throwline is attached to the left-hand stile, at least 25 cm from the top. This is flicked over a cleat on the right-hand stile of the next flat. The throwline is then pulled tight, passed under a cleat near the foot of the first flat and finally wound tightly round the lower cleat of the second flat. A flat standing alone or unsupported at one side is held in position by a stage brace.

[STILE]

open end of eyelet

large eyelets – one opened to make hook

wing bolt with nuts to tighten brace – weld nut on angle

two mild steel angle brackets for slide – lower one screwed down.

allow narrow gap for slide

set wire handle in wet concrete

38×38 mm hardwood

shape from mild steel

Adjustable brace.

Making braces and weights

hinged

square weight

mortice and tenon joint or simple screwing of brace to sides

French brace.

stage screw as an alternative to weight (not suitable for hall floors or rostra tops)

set wire mesh in concrete

wood block

cord

card or board

Making the weights

Weights (and braces) can be hired or purchased from stage suppliers but easy, cheap weights can be made as illustrated. The round weight should be approximately 25 cm in diameter × 10 cm high. The square weight 30 × 15 × 15 cm – the gap will be 8 × 3 cm to allow the brace to pass underneath. The concrete mixture should be 1 part cement, 2 parts sand and 3 parts aggregate (gravel or crushed stone). Use three quarters of one part water.

150 × 18 mm plank or board

wood block for gap

Other flat supports . . .

main batten

wing nut
main batten
coach bolt
steel 'U' section
flat

Hang-irons for 'flying' flats.

wing flats can be supported and reversed on pivots – a double-sided canvas flat (above left) is held by a 'U' section, the wing curtain is attached to a pivoted runner (above, centre).

Flats can be joined by hinge, wood block or cleats.

Two small free-standing flats can be supported by angle brackets and weighted with concrete blocks, bricks, etc.

screw or nail

Small independent flats and screens can be supported by small French braces, hinged to the stiles.

If a small free-standing flat is needed and braces are not available, a quick method of support is a 50 × 25 mm timber from the side of another secure flat. But this will prevent access behind the small flat.

fold for stovage

A simple screen background consisting of three or four flats

To give maximum clearance between front and rear, the supports can be carried across the top rails as shown. The braces behind the back flats can be of the French or sliding brace type.

This kind of simple setting could be useful in a school hall as a screen for Nativity and Passion plays – see pages 240–242.

batten link between two flats secured with metal bracket and wooden blade

blade
bracket

75 × 25mm batten link between flats screwed down to top of rails – an alternative fixing is shown in inset.

BACKSTAGE

fixed brace

extending brace

When flats are interlocked for box-style settings ensure that they overlap as shown here in order to avoid backstage light penetrating.

BACKSTAGE

'return' from flat 'A'
'return' from flat 'B'
(see glossary)

A

B

Ground-rows and cut-out borders

Large ground-rows are flats in a horizontal position on the floor of the stage with a profile of hills, trees, etc. cut out in plywood or hardboard and attached to the upper edge. See page 117 for an illustration.

The smaller ground-rows can be made entirely of plywood or hardboard with one or two strengtheners of 50×25 mm timber.

Thin plywood or hardboard tacked and glued to the top edge of the flat. This can be removed later so that the flat can be used for other purposes.

a set-piece supported with French brace

3 mm. material (plywood)

bracing as required

screw to box

crates and boxes make useful supports for low ground rows - useful also as small rostra

part of old flat adapted for use as a hinged extension to ground row.

58

tied to flies/batten   main battens

LIGHTING BATTEN

BORDER

cut-out borders

'leg' between wing and border

Cut-out borders are constructed in much the same way for wings and borders.
Cut-outs and ground-rows are ideal for pantomime and similar productions.

cut-out on wings

canvas cut-out using
gauze for large gaps

ground row

footlights

WING

hinged as book flat

Doors and door frames

All doors opening offstage require only one side covered in canvas and painted.

canvas or hardboard both sides-painted 'planks'

hardboard or 3 mm plywood reveal-nail to stile

ball catch

saw slot

DOOR

peg through door

sliding wooden bolt for rustic door

metal ties

iron sill

frames all 75 × 25 mm

1 The easiest way of hanging a door is to hinge it direct to the flat opening – a strip of canvas behind the door will exclude backstage light.

2 A hardboard 'reveal' about 20 cm deep, nailed round the opening, will give an appearance of solidity. The back edges can be strengthened with 50 × 25 mm battens. Door stops or moulding (thin vertical 35 × 10 mm wood strips) will exclude light from backstage.

3 A more substantial version of **2**: the reveal is built of 20 × 2.5 cm planking and fastened to the flat with small metal brackets.

door stop

Rear (backstage).

3 mm moulding stop

Rear (backstage).

25 mm moulding
door stop

Rear (backstage).

Independent frame & doors

cross section through frame

12 mm wood frame

3 mm plywood or hardboard

metal ties and angle

eyelet for brace

various for all flat door voids

all door stops of 25×25 mm softwood

mouldings of polystyrene strip, card or stiff paper

FLAT

200× 18 mm reveal

double sill

screwed ends of sills to reveal

12/18 mm fascia in plywood or softwood

independant frame

overhanging cornice

flat

Front (on stage).

Rear (backstage).

61

A frame for all purposes – door or window

glue and screw or nail corner blocks

nail lintel to post

post

18 to 25 mm thickness

from 150 mm for small openings to 250 mm for large doors or archways

2 iron sills screwed to bottom sides of posts

Basic structure.

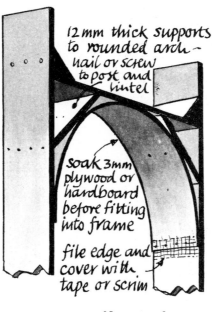

12 mm thick supports to rounded arch – nail or screw to post and lintel

soak 3mm plywood or hardboard before fitting into frame

file edge and cover with tape or scrim

Norman archway.

saw half-way through and tape before fitting

glue and nail to support

Gothic archway.

roundels for door on right can be: a) sawn cardboard roll, b) polystyrene block, c) cardboard shapes taped together.

Window opening.

metal angle brackets secure 'false' lintel

wooden sill – fit where required with brackets

The variations are wide – the only limitation is that of dimension.

Gothic door with solid moulding.

arches shaped from 75 mm softwood pieces or 3mm ply shapes

French window.

if pulley system is attempted use 25mm thick frame and small pulley

25 x 25 mm wood frame

sash weights hidden behind flats to each side of window

A basic frame is useful if it has been designed to fit the door void of an existing flat. The change from one type of door or window to another is quite simple provided that care is taken with the means of attachment. A sash window, as illustrated on the right, would require four holes to carry sashes with weights. Since pulleys cannot conveniently be fitted into this type of frame, smooth grooves should be carefully made in the holes to carry the cords.

Sash window.

parting bead - 25 x 12 mm.

WINDOW
VOID

moulding –
75×25 mm

a *The illustration shows a
half-section through
window-frame.*

Windows

a This is an independent window with a frame designed to fit an existing window flat. The frame can be fitted with a casement, as shown, or with a sash (see previous page).

b A small window opening without frame or glass: it has been built into a modified existing stock flat, using a hardboard reveal and a 150×25 mm wood plank sill. A 50×25 mm batten under the front edge of the sill will eliminate the light crack.

c and **d** Two methods of creating leaded windows: painting lines on film or taping. Taping can be quicker and cheaper. The small inset in **d** shows the taping of a casement window, whereas the main illustration shows taping to the edge of the reveal where the window does not have to open.

e A small stained glass window.

Joints for the casement frame are illustrated below.

TOP RAIL

alternative joint at corners

STILE

100 mm wide hardboard reveal - soak in water before bending

ON STAGE SIDE

canvas tabs glued over hardboard reveal

cross section of sill - 150 × 25 mm plank

75 × 25 mm rail of flat

50 × 25 mm to add thickness to sill

b *A small window opening built to represent a semi-circular light in a stone wall: the canvas is pulled taut over the edge of the reveal by glueing tabs firmly. (See page 119 for a similar shape in a setting for 'The Merchant of Venice'.)*

c *Windows requiring many 'leads' can be effectively simulated by painting lines (about 1 cm wide) on clear or frosted thin P.V.C. or P.V.A. sheeting. Note the fixing method.*

transparent film

card strip

thumb tacks

oil paint for lines - use a straight edge

ON STAGE SIDE

canvas

d *Rear view of a lozenge-shaped leaded window, using 10 or 15 mm black tape as an alternative to painting on film.*

OFF STAGE SIDE

equal spacing

thumb tacks

film

coloured tissues for glass

oil-paint for lines

e *A stained glass window. The 'leads' are painted on transparent film. The coloured glass is simulated by overlaying coloured tissue paper on the back side with clear varnish. The colours can be enriched by adding more layers of tissue.*

65

SCREENS: A concertina screen

Where funds or facilities will not allow backcloths and you are seeking an alternative method of scene-changing, a pair – or more – of book flats (page 51) can be used, hinged together as shown. This assembly shows, at one end, a firm fixing to a post by butt-hinges and, on the other, a French brace.

Such a screen is used in a production of 'She Stoops to Conquer' – see the section on design, page 97.

screen can be pulled out for straight wall or folded to any angle

two halves of a rising butt hinge – available in left or right hand turns

small spigot castors in rail of flat, large spigot in wood block

If the flats employed are double-sided canvas or board, the screen can be folded, reversed in the closed position and re-fastened to display another scene. In such a case the prongs of butt hinges must be attached at both ends at the same spacing and height.

French brace

wood block or castor equal to gap

angle bracket
POST
butt hinge
canvas strip
FLAT.1

canvas strip on hinge side
FLAT 2
FLAT 3
ball castor

glue & tack a skirt of canvas to conceal castors and gap under screen

stage weight

Arched screens

one reveal slightly raised to pass over the other

narrow archway

wide archway

always keep this flat at slight angle to archway to aid stability

The archway shown offers a wide range of shape by opening and closing the 'book'. A French brace hinged to the third flat ensures stability.

STEP LADDER

360° turn on flats by double webbing

This set of three flats includes a doorway and a window opening. Two flats can be easily folded through 90° to create a new spatial concept. The method of fixing to a vertical structure is again by rising butt hinges. An example of this type of screen can be noticed in the scenes and plan drawing for 'The Merchant of Venice', positioned upstage right – see pages 92–93. For a more detailed close-up of the painted surface turn to page 119.

Sliding screens

If curtains are not available, or backcloths are in short supply, a possible solution is to make up a set of hardboard screens. They can be made to any height and width. A running track allows for easy movement.

jig-saw cutting over space between tables

felt or fibre-tip marker drawn along T-square or straight edge

hardboard

either ball, roller or plastic runners or small castors

'G' clamps whilst gluing

temporary batten until glue hardens

frame - glue and nail battens to hardboard

SOFTWOOD SECTIONS

Listed right in diagrammatic layout are various metric wood sections. Those shown in solid black are mentioned on pages concerned with the manufacture of rostra and flats. Remember that planed timber will always measure less than sawn sizes (nominal sizes). Allowance should be made for this when calculating requirements. Plywood can be obtained in 3, 4, 6, 9, 12 and 18 mm thicknesses. Thicker sheets are not required. Dowelling is available in 3, 4, 6, 9, 12, 15, 18 and 22 mm diameters.

TOP TRACK
two 100 × 32 mm battens screwed to top plate
75 × 25 mm screen frame
hardboard
16 mm thick

This assembly shows a set of cut-out screens set out approximately 1 metre in front of the cyclorama or backcloth – used with strong back lighting. This method offers a variety of changes by means of a simple track system. When the screens are drawn back into the wings they reveal the scene painted on the backcloth or the cyclorama. Four, five or more can stretch over any width of stage provided that there is enough track for easy movement. The cut-outs may be varied to suit the needs of the play – this assembly was designed to show New York at night in a production of 'West Side Story' – see also the section on design, pages 105–106.

BOTTOM TRACK
a slight forward lean to screens to rest against top track
runners
3 mm plywood
25 × 25 mm wood strips
STAGE/HALL FLOOR

height of screens is determined by borders

thickness in millimetres	width in millimetres				
	25	50	75	100	125
16	■	■	▭	▭	▭
19	▭	▭	▭	▭	▭
25	■	■	■	■	▭
32	▭	▭	▭	■	▭
50	▭	■	■	■	▭

thickness in millimetres	width in millimetres			
	150	175	200	225
18	▭	▭	■	▭
25	■	▭	■	▭
38	▭	▭	▭	▭
50	■	▭	▭	▭
75	▭	▭	■ ← main battens	

Scenes from 'Fiddler on the Roof'. Top: the kitchen of Tevye's house, the furniture removed to show more clearly the construction of the revolving truck (see page 46). Bottom left and right: the truck reversed to positions S.L. and S.R., offering exterior views of Tevye's house. In the yard scene on the left, fencing has been joined to the house to create a different silhouette effect – see page 149 for fencing. The scene on the right shows the house shape slightly modified by adding a rostrum truck – see page 42 – resembling a log pile against the wall. A ground row conceals the batten lighting for the cyclorama.

Design

PLANNING · MODELS · WORKING DRAWINGS · TYPES OF DESIGN

SOME NOTES ON DESIGN

The planning and work required for any production depend on the time, energy and facilities available. Ideas may be simplified to meet a tight schedule. On the other hand, a very elaborate design is not necessarily more demanding (or rewarding) than a very simple one. The empty space that will become the acting area must always be considered in relation to good proportion within that space.

It is useful to consider a few approaches to the matter of design:

a If we think about the empty space, we begin to think in three dimensions, so that the setting and all the parts that go to make the setting will be conceived in 3-D.

b Balance must be achieved between the main planes (surfaces) and lines, the texture of the materials and the colour of paint and costumes.

c The placing of the parts and properties must always be related to the acting area and allow for the free movement of the actors.

It is important to stress the word 'balance' because this characteristic of good design can be overlooked if too much attention is given to detail or the less important parts of the setting. Always work from the whole concept – the large spatial areas and masses – and then develop the smaller details: the textural effects and colour within this framework.

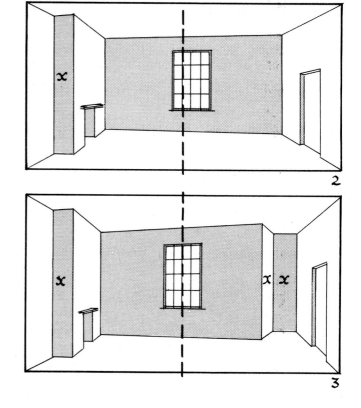

2

3

Balance should not be confused with symmetry, which is an exact correspondence of parts on either side of a centre line or axis – see **1** below.

In a simple setting with three walls, a floor and a ceiling (a box set) a completely symmetrical arrangement can be very dull and uninteresting.

A slight shift of emphasis from the central kind of balance can be achieved by moving the flats slightly, introducing a niche or chimney breast, for example, using quite narrow flats like **x** in **2** and **3**. This kind of balance offers much more variety to the eye. The sketch model on page 77 and perspective view on page 81 illustrate the point more clearly.

But symmetry does have a valuable part to play in many design ideas, especially in more elaborate, decorative settings. Provided that a wide variety of shape, pattern and tonal contrast are included, more or less symmetrical design can be quite satisfactory – see the setting on pages 84 and 85.

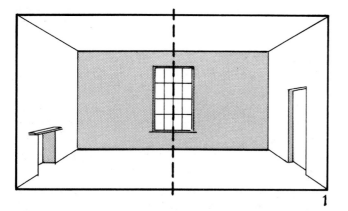

1

Some design terms

Certain terms used in design are introduced in this section:

Decorative design is related primarily to the painted scenery of backcloths, wings and borders; also to pattern and ornament within the setting.

Textural ideas relate to an interest in the surface appearance or 'feel' of the surfaces – often without the colour associated with more decorative designs.

The term *tonal* refers to the lightness or darkness of an area or surface, of whatever colour or texture, and is important when aiming for contrast or similarity between the parts of a setting.

The terms *decorative*, *textural* and *tonal* are usually related to the two-dimensional effects of painted canvas or the broken surfaces of paint.

When a design is more three-dimensional in concept, the term *structural* is used. This term expresses well the use of surfaces that suggest volume and solidity and where structures are erected and then covered with various materials. Settings of this kind can often employ new materials such as expanded polystyrene sheet and block, all kinds of metal foils and plasters. One major advantage of this type of scenery over the traditional painted scene is the range of possibilities it offers for imaginative lighting. When oblique lighting strikes across a built-up textural surface a much stronger sense of depth is achieved.

These terms apply equally to the section on painting (see pages 118–123 for surface painting, 128–131 for 3-D effects).

Reading, discussion and research

The design for a setting depends on a number of factors. It must meet the requirements of the text, the playwright's directions and the director's concept of the play.

To meet the demands of the text requires careful reading of the play and the stage directions, both at the beginning of each scene and throughout the text, so that the basic theme and the mood can be absorbed from scene to scene. The designer has then to develop and expand his own concept with the director.

Sometimes, when a playwright gives a detailed description of the setting, it can be more inhibiting than a simple word or phrase that describes only the location – 'the blasted heath', for example. Remember that your own concept, whilst being true to the playwright's needs, must not be submerged by too detailed a description. Always try to develop your own ideas round the main theme and location of the play.

Whatever the play, its location, time and period, it will always be necessary to do some research. Delve into background material from any source. You can use your local reference library, the museum, paintings, architectural features, costume books and personal recollections.

The director's understanding of the text must be discussed in detail and a common approach to all problems agreed. As the first sketches and notes are considered and discussed between director and designer, certain differences will become apparent – especially if the visual imagination of the two is not in accord. A design scheme has then to be developed to resolve any major differences.

Provided that the designer considers certain basic requirements of the acting area *before* sketching out his design the differences between designer and director are likely to be slight. The considerations are these:

Firstly, know your space. Are the exits and entrances in the right position for ideal movement of the cast, or will you have to introduce a new entrance? (See also the question of placing temporary stages – page 83.)

Secondly, the correct placing of the seating arrangements on stage and the careful positioning of properties and supports that could trip up the actors during certain moves.

Thirdly, considerable care to be exercised in the positions of lights – discussed in detail in the section on stage lighting.

Finally, think always of the basic limitations of the actual building. Is there sufficient headroom for a balcony? Will a large 'prop' fit within the narrow confines between the existing wings? Is there adequate dressing room space for quick changes of elaborate costumes?

Always plan carefully and relate visual concepts to the space and the facilities available.

PLANNING THE SET

There are as many approaches to planning a setting as there are designers, but a few methods are frequently used:

1 the sketch method; 2 notes and rough sketches; 3 the rough model; 4 settings in a model theatre. These methods may overlap but they will now, for convenience, be considered separately.

Presetting - Quayside

ships' masts

back lighting only

A1,S1 Street (or Quayside) (use either pre-setting or this)

hinged flats opened out

ramp →

A1,S2 - Belmont

drapes in front of cyc.

great candle-sticks

A2,S2 - Shylock's House - Street

large house cut-out

move ramp S.R.?

A2,S4 - Another Street

fountain

A2,S7 - Casket scene - Belmont

drapes

caskets

cyc. covered with dark drapes

bench

throne

drapes slightly drawn

← hinged flat open

canvas cut-out arcade

'The Merchant of Venice' – Shakespeare.

The eight sketches illustrate major scene and lighting changes.

This is an example of the first stage of planning the set using the sketch method. Three of the scenes based on these sketches are shown on pages 92 and 93.

1 The sketch method

Many designers prefer to draw a series of small sketches, usually executed in line or pen and wash, to show all the basic shape and structure and the effect of lighting on each scene.

The series of sketches on the opposite page are for the scene changes in a production of Shakespeare's 'Merchant of Venice'.

Executed in pen and ink only, the tonal effects are made by 'hatching' (a series of close lines) and help to show the director and lighting technician the basic concept of contrasts from scene to scene.

The sketches shown could as well have been executed in pen and wash or even with touches of colour – wash is quicker in application and gives a more 'fluid' effect.

Experiment with various media – pen, pen and wash, cut papers, watercolour and gouache or any other agreeable medium.

What must always be remembered is that the technique employed should suit the designer.

Notes in and around the sketches should give all necessary information on set changes and make clear the acting area.

2 Notes and rough sketches

Another method is to jot down everything that occurs to you as you read the text and talk with the director. This will make less demand on drawing ability and facilities but will require notes that are highly detailed – giving information to the director and all those concerned in the production.

Research should be undertaken and notes on colour, materials and lighting (together with samples) can be usefully attached to the main notes.

Very simple sketches of the elevation and plan view (explained on pages 79 and 81) will be helpful to clarify all written notes.

The quick sketch plan and elevation shown here with notes illustrate a starting point for planning a setting for Richard Rodney Bennett's 'All the King's Men'.

'All the King's Men' - Richard Rodney Be[nnett]

Scene - The walls and main gate outside the City of Gloucester
Backing - Either a painted backcloth or cyc. with ground row. Glimpse of river Severn into distance - few trees in mid-distance.

Director wants part of wall as high as possible so that citizens of Gloucester look down on King Charles' men - suggest building high platform C.S behind wall over a scaffold framework.

painted cloth or cyc?
walls of hardboard
large double doors
ladder up to high platf[orm]
S.R. ELEVATION 'All the King's Me[n]

2 metre high platform
cyc →
tower
ground row
main gate
Charles' tent
Orchestra to left of auditorium.
Rough plan - All the King's Men

line of imagined river Severn
City area
Humpty Dumpty (if used)
2/3 small rostra →
High gro[und] tent

Machine - The enormous mechanism (Humpty Dumpty) suggested only by introducing a spar or two of wood at high level - or just noise of

General placement of levels, river, etc. Allow space S.R for Humpty D. [...]

75

3 The rough model

Some designers prefer to draw a scale elevation of the setting on stiff paper or thin card, cutting out the parts with tabs and sticking to a base with some rough indications of colour.

Conventional box set

The illustration shows the scaled layout for making up a rough model. Draw up on thin card or stiff cartridge paper, colouring all parts *before* cutting to avoid the curling of the card.

Note that a group of flats (e.g. 3–5) can, for convenience, be cut out as one piece. The sketch below shows the linking up of three groups (1–8).

paint before cutting

fold lines

1   2   3 4 5   6 7 8

door backing

window backing

9   10   11   12   pattern wall   brick wall

fire   chair   fold

bed cover

layout for 'Lunch Hour' – John Mortimer.

curve and glue 6 over 8

8   5   7   6   4 3   2   1

tabs glued to base

Rear view of flats 1 to 8.

fold mantelshelf down

glue together

REAR

fold fender up

Small props may be cut from thin pieces of card or balsa wood.

Prepare a piece of cardboard, thin plywood or hardboard for a base and draw out a ground plan showing positions for walls, etc. Place model scenery and props in position and colour floor, mats and other additions.

THICK CARD OR BOARD FOR BASE GROUND PLAN

FIRE 3

6

7 8

4

5

9

2

10

11

BED

CHAIR

1

HOUSE TABS

PROSCENIUM

SETTING LINE

12

BALSA WOOD FOR 'PROPS'

BOSTIK No 1

STEEL STRAIGHT EDGE FOR CUTTING

4 Settings in a model theatre

The method most closely related to the actual stage setting is that using a scale model theatre – such models often have a lighting system based on a transformer and mains supply.

The setting within the scale model theatre shown below is a scene from 'Aladdin', showing the cave. A photograph of the setting and lighting effect is shown on page 87.

joint, glue and screw all the framework

5×5 mm

rail for 'flying' the scenery

3 mm plywood for cyclorama and proscenium

all framework in 20×10 mm hardwood

CYCLORAMA

'BACKCLOTH'- NOT IN USE

scenery battens

lighting battens in compartments or individual lamps

PROSCENIUM

lighting batten for cyclorama (sky) if required

notched rails - 30×10 mm

floor of stage approx. 6mm thick

wires tacked along frame

BACKCLOTH

WING Nº3

WING 2

WING 1

master switch for transformer

scenery cut from stiff card

4 switches to lighting battens: compartment battens built from balsa wood, individual lamps (spots) can use old torch reflectors. fit 'gels' to all lamps

proscenium arch 30×60cm maximum - use false proscenium to make smaller.

16 × 100 mm softwood base to house the wires and transformer

to mains supply

THE WORKING DRAWINGS

Following the planning stage, it is useful to prepare working drawings before building complicated sets. (Simple cloth and border settings may not require such drawings.)

1 When one of the sketches or models has been agreed upon, the *ground-plan* is prepared.

The ground-plan is a top or bird's eye view of the floor of the stage showing all horizontal members of the parts of flats and other units. The plan will show the area of the stage, the position of the proscenium and of the cyclorama and the width of each flat. Also

shown are the direction of door openings, curtains and exits.

2 To prepare your ground-plan, make sure that you have the correct measurements of the stage area. Note positions of all projections from walls, pillars or columns on the floor, girders overhead and anything else that juts into the stage area.

3 When all main dimensions are drawn on the plan in a scale of 4 cm to 1 m (1 : 25), plot the exact positions of the flats, rostra, cloths, curtains and other items relevant to the setting from the

setting-line.

This line is related to the track-line of the front tabs. If front tabs are not being used, the setting line may be brought forward, on to the apron if there is one.

The important thing is to have a useful guide line. The centre-line (CL on the illustration below) makes a right-angle with the setting-line. Those concerned with the construction of the set can mark these lines on the stage itself – and work from them.

Ground plan for a box setting: plan for 'The Living Room' by Graham Greene

THE WORKING DRAWINGS
(continued)

4 The *elevation* or *section* drawings show the vertical and upright parts of your setting. The height of flats and rostra can be indicated to scale – widths are accurate, but it must be remembered that widths appear to vary, according to the angle from which they are viewed.

The elevation is taken through the centre-line of the stage (CL) as if sliced through the axis.

A *front* elevation can be useful in certain settings but more often a perspective view will, together with plan and elevation, provide better information, both to the director and to those involved in building the set.

5 Another useful drawing is one that offers elevation drawings of all the flats and units to be used. Each flat or unit is numbered to correspond with numbers marked on the ground-plan.

Elevation – towards stage left.

Perspective view.

Elevation of flats used in this setting.

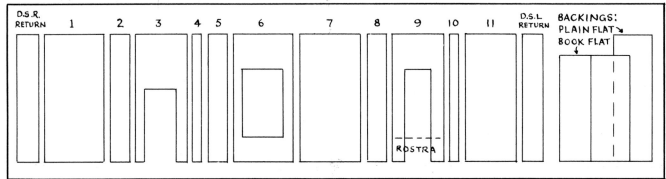

Useful symbols for plans

Working drawings showing a scaled plan need to show the flats, units and properties within the setting. If certain symbols are used (especially useful in box-sets containing much furniture) they will be helpful to the director and to those reponsible for placing properties.

Illustrated here are the conventional and essential symbols used on ground-plans and elevations. You may need to make up a few symbols of your own if unusual features are introduced, e.g. an outcrop of rock or a chariot.

The stage outline

The plan view.

The elevation or section drawing.

Rostra

Two sizes of rostra (note diagonals to distinguish from tables).

 UP

Steps – with an arrow and UP to indicate direction.

Cloths

curtains (tabs)

backcloths

borders
(*items above stage level shown by dash*)

Flats

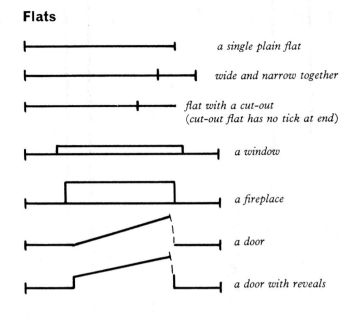

a single plain flat

wide and narrow together

flat with a cut-out
(*cut-out flat has no tick at end*)

a window

a fireplace

a door

a door with reveals

a bay, or niche

a bay window

Properties

tables

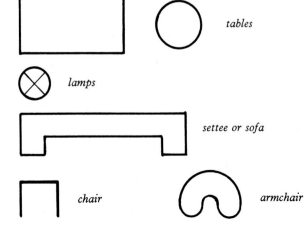

lamps

settee or sofa

chair

armchair

TYPES OF STAGE DESIGN

Previous pages have been concerned with ways of planning a setting. The next pages in this section deal with different types of setting, from the simplest to the more elaborate.

It is hoped that these notes and illustrations will stimulate ideas and provide possible starting points for designer, director and others concerned with various backstage activities.

The types of setting can be conveniently grouped as follows:

1 *Arena* and *theatre-in-the-round* (including *open or thrust stages* – these stages are often portable or adaptable rostra-type staging.)

2 *Screen settings*.

3 *Curtain* – the most common, frequently found in school or college halls.

4 *Wing and cloth* – painted cloth sets.

5 *Box sets* – permanent or semi-permanent usually.

6 *Cyclorama* – where the skycloth plays an important part in the setting.

7 *Composite settings* – three or more confined acting areas in one setting, usually at different levels.

8 *Permanent or semi-permanent structures* – a 'built' set often of many levels with balcony, steps, etc.

It will be seen that certain of the plays illustrated could be suitably placed under an alternative group, e.g. a cyclorama setting can also be 'permanent', but the point to note is that 'cyclorama' is the spur to the design concept whereas the permanency of the setting is the direct result of meeting the demands of a particular play.

1 Arena and theatre-in-the-round

Perhaps the simplest of settings, certainly from the point of view of scenery, is the arena or theatre-in-the-round. The audience is grouped on three or on all sides, with the seating arranged higher than the stage or with the stage slightly above the level of the audience.

'The Importance of Being Earnest' by Oscar Wilde.

The model shown above illustrates the basic simplicity of the design – the only decorative feature being the two screens. The curtain (a screen or flats could have been used) is to hide players, sound and lighting equipment and for quick changing purposes.

The problem in this particular production of 'The Importance of Being Earnest' was to stage it in a long narrow hall for a one-night stand. This involved the transporting of the rostra stage, lighting equipment, curtains, screens and costumes.

The problem of making the production work in the narrow hall (15 × 6 m) can be seen from the small sketch-plan made on the site beforehand:

It was impossible to arrange the stage at either of the narrow ends because of the positions of the main entrance and emergency exit. The solution was to set the stage against the centre of the long wall facing the main entrance, leaving a minimum space backstage of half a metre and grouping the audience on three sides. (The method of fixing a curtain against the ceiling in a matter of minutes is shown on page 22.)

Two screens were used to give some sense of change to the scenes. They were painted on both sides, were interchangeable and could be used singly or not at all. The photograph below shows one of the screens, with the curtain fitted against the ceiling.

Thrust or open settings

Another simple basic setting can be the open rostra-and-steps stage backed by curtains, cloths or a simple cut-out screen – with curtained openings, entrances and exits.

The sketch plan shown here shows a typical thrust stage arrangement – the outer lines represent the confines of the hall.

Sketch plan for 'Henry IV Part 1'.

The setting for 'Henry IV Part 1' is basically a protruding or thrust stage with an Elizabethan style of backing, built as a permanent structure from wood and hardboard. The openings are curtained in a patterned fabric printed by stencil (see page 122 for methods of stencilling.)

The problem of staging this production was the inconvenience of a comparatively low ceiling. So the upper storey shown in the illustrations on the next page had to be purely decorative in this particular hall. Obviously, if height allowed, the upper windows and balcony would be put to use, with a platform and steps behind the screen.

The use of lower rostra downstage left and right created another level for grouping the actors. The change of location was effected by banners and cut-outs raised in the centre upstage, between the 'walls' of the wood and hardboard structure.

A useful device to aid unity of design between upstage and downstage is shown in the relationship between the railings in the centre of the backing and the railings containing the lower rostra downstage.

Right: a three-quarter view of the scale model showing the first row of seating and the aisles at the sides of the stage which are useful storage for properties not in use.

Below: the actual setting. Note the murals at the sides (see pages 117 for details).

Act III Scene 1: A room in Sir Peter Teazle's house ('The School for Scandal').
Another example of a symmetrical type of set using large movable screens with a fixed central false proscenium. The screens can be adapted from old flats.

Act IV Scene 1: The Picture Room.
All the same screens rearranged and the proscenium screen revealed to show an inset scene. The mirror over the fireplace alters the appearance and the pediment over the window is removed.

2 Screen settings

Where sufficient curtains, flats and other scenery are not readily available or where a quick-change method of scene changing is desirable, screens can fulfil the requirements.

Screens, in pairs, threes or fours can occasionally be found and be altered by re-covering and repainting. Where very large screens are needed book flats can be built up from existing flats.

With a screen on either side of the acting area, the back can be filled by simply building a wooden frame between the screens – usually rather higher to make a focal point. Either curtains or another screen can be fitted behind the frame giving the effect of a false proscenium. Or both curtains and screen can be used if a change of setting is required.

The two scenes shown here come from a production of 'The School for Scandal'. The two side screens are changed or switched and the curtains drawn back to alter the setting.

Further variations between scenes can be effected by interchanging pediments over the false proscenium. Tongues of wood are equally spaced on each pediment to slot into a pair of brackets behind the proscenium.

A

HALF CURTAIN
HALF CYCLORAMA
(BACK WALL)

ROSTRUM AND
STEPS

B

PAINTED BACKCLOTH

C

CYCLORAMA
(OR BACKCLOTH)

CUT-OUT

GROUND ROW

D

3 Curtain sets

Curtain setting is the most elementary and frequent type of existing setting.

It is found in most schools, colleges and church halls, serving as a general backing for assemblies of one kind or another and is ideal for this purpose.

Unfortunately, curtain settings are often the only backing for the annual play – and can be dull when no flats or rostra are available.

What can be done with curtains alone? Illustration **A** shows a curtain set typical of most schools, the traditional setting of three or sometimes four pairs of curtain wings, a back-curtain divided in the centre which can be drawn back and a pair of front tabs (curtains) set just within the proscenium frame. Three or four curtain borders correspond to the pairs of wings.

Try pushing back the upstage curtains into the wings and seeing what the back wall offers in the way of a cyclorama. Perhaps it is a clean, light and smooth surface and only needs a few lights to bring it to life. If this can be achieved, you have a cyclorama set with wing curtains.

Illustration **B** shows one half of the back curtain drawn back with a simple step and rostra.

A curtain set in conjunction with a painted backcloth can be most rewarding. If funds allow, two backcloths may be used, the back traverse tabs being drawn across while the cloths are changed. If there is no fly space above the stage, cloths can be rolled on a cylinder of wood (see page 23 for description). Illustration **C** shows this type of setting.

A curtain set combined with ground-rows or cut-outs and backcloth (or plain cyclorama) adds yet more variety. Cut-outs and ground-rows are described on pages 51 and 58 – small cut-outs that are low and not too wide can be attached to boxes or simple wooden brackets. Illustration **D** shows this arrangement.

If the wing curtains are on swivels (see pages 18 and 19), there can be a colour change on the reverse side.

4 Wing and cloth sets

Pantomime, revue, light operetta and all productions demanding a touch of fantasy benefit from the use of colourful decorative scenery. It is in this sphere of stage design that the painted canvas and occasionally gauze – the traditional wing and cloth setting – is most suitable. Little or no construction is required apart from the occasional rostra and at least two sets of steps or a simple staircase.

The scenes are conveyed in depth by means of plain or, more frequently, cut-out canvas wings and borders.

Gauze is used to support any large holes cut out of the canvas wings (see page 24 for the use of gauze on canvas). Each wing and border takes the eye back to the tour-de-force upstage – the painted backcloth. Very often a strong illusion of depth is achieved by these simple means.

The illustration below shows a scene from a scale model setting for Aladdin's cave. The only construction is a large treasure chest and a cut-out of a rock-like shape. (This scene is also shown in position within the model theatre on page 78.)

5 Box sets – 1

If the text of the play demands an interior setting with a strong sense of realism, then the box setting is ideal. Constructed from flats and usually with a 'ceiling' of suspended flats (although borders often replace the ceiling), the box set is only practical if a suitable quantity of flats is available. For example, the setting below would require between 20 and 30 depending on the widths used.

The playwright's directions for 'Look Back in Anger' are detailed and require careful study. The ceiling of the attic room has a marked slope: decisions have to be taken as to whether it is practical to build such a ceiling from flats. Borders may have to be substituted. But the dormer windows downstage right must be included to give the feel of an attic.

The lighting presents many interesting problems. A landing with a skylight seen through a long oblong window in the room is called for – this can be omitted but is worth aiming at. The lights for the dormers are essential and should be strongly lit.

Ground plan for 'Look Back in Anger'

Look Back in Anger

The two illustrations on the right show the scale model setting. The ceiling plays a very prominent part in the design. Note how the shapes of each wall are affected by the long slope above – the back wall by its angle and the side walls by the marked contrast in height. Another interesting design feature is the shape made by the dormer windows into the ceiling area.

Note also that border batten lighting is useless in this type of setting – all light sources must be supplied from perches immediately behind the proscenium and from F.O.H. (front of house, the auditorium area). Intense local sources will be floods or concentrated spots behind the windows (see page 188 of the section on lighting).

In an old attic room one can imagine that the state of the ceiling and walls will have been neglected. Textural effects can be introduced to create the correct atmosphere (see pages 118–122 of the section on painting).

BOX SETTING for 'Look Back in Anger' by John Osborne. Act I Scene 1: Day.

Act II: Night.

Box sets – 2

Sometimes a play demanding realistic treatment needs two or more interiors. This gives an opportunity to build a box-within-a-box type of setting. Such is the case with 'Bernadette' by Noël Woolf and Sheila Buckley.

Three interiors are needed, all quite different in style and character: a disused prison room; a well-appointed study and an austere convent room.

The stage available was of average size and with plenty of space for 'flying' scenery – and there were plenty of flats available.

The ground plan and the three photographs show how three box sets were arranged, one inside another – the whole stage area being gradually revealed (rather like peeling away the skins of an onion). In another play, also requiring three scenes, this process might be reversed – adding a box within a box. And if all flats can be 'flown' the scenes can succeed each other in any order.

The ground plan, when related carefully to each of the three scenes, explains how each scene was pre-arranged at the start of the play. Three types of line have been used to make the plan clearer. Note how the wall on S.L. ('Stage Left' when facing the audience) was used in both Acts II and III but received a change of emphasis by the drape over the door and the pictures on the wall.

Act I: The cachot – a disused prison in Lourdes.

3-in-1 box set: ground plan for 'Bernadette'

Act II:
The Dean of Lourdes'
study –
note the drape on the
door S.L. and the
position of the wall S.L.

Ceiling flats were omitted in this production, black borders being used instead. Note how a wide range of lighting is employed to help create different localities. In Act I the light descends mainly from batten No. 1 S.L. In Act II the windows bring in intense light from a row of four 1000w floods. In Act III the ground-row lights pick out the cyclorama. (Ground-row refers to scenery and to lighting – see page 176 for lighting.)

Act III:
The convent at
Nevers –
note change of the S.L.
wall and the way it
ties in with the
new backing.

6 Cyclorama sets

A cyclorama set is basically a setting of curtain wings or wing flats, with the upstage area entirely backed by the skycloth – which sometimes curves downstage at the sides. The whole acting space can be framed by the proscenium arch but the concept of a large open sky area and wings is quite valid without the use of a proscenium provided that the 'sky' is itself framed.

The scenic constructions most suitable for cyclorama settings are rather skeletal – the more 'bones' or linear structure, the more interesting the silhouettes. It is immediately evident how important this type of setting is in the scenes shown here from 'The Merchant of Venice'.

Note how the setting has been deliberately opened out, pushing the architecture to both sides of the stage but tying them together by the use of steps enveloping the whole stage area.

In the opening scene the harbour is achieved by the use of three verticals and a cross-piece to indicate ships and a rather stumpy cylinder for a capstan.

The importance of the cyclorama to set off this scene can be clearly seen.

Act I Scene 1: The harbour scene from 'The Merchant of Venice'.

In the ground plan below note the use of a wide variety of mobile pivoted flats to achieve maximum variety between the various scenes. The mobile screen marked 'A' on the ground plan is shown on page 67 of the section on flats.

**Ground plan for 'The Merchant of Venice'
A cyclorama set with mobile pivoted flats**

Both scenes here rely strongly upon the cyclorama, only the court scene making use of the softening effect of curtains for an interior. Note how the canvas frame arcade (illustration right) links the two sides of the setting.

Note the use of a ramp in this rostra-stage setting – it allows the cast to use the auditorium gangways for their entrances and exits, which can greatly enliven the movement of the players.

Right: Act V Scene 1: The garden scene, Belmont. Note the small half-arch at one end of the arcade in relation to the previous scene.

Below: Act IV Scene 1: A court of justice.

See page 127 for curtain printing, page 153 for throne construction, pages 40–41 for steps.

7 Composite settings

Settings requiring two or more rooms or other locations simultaneously are termed composite sets. Such acting areas are sometimes used together, at other times separately. Areas not in use are usually blacked out or masked by gauzes. For example, 'The Diary of Anne Frank' and 'Five Finger Exercise' require rooms only; 'Under Milk Wood' requires rooms and exterior locations.

Another play requiring a composite set is Arthur Miller's 'Death of a Salesman' which demands three rooms and a surrounding, dream-like, exterior.

The illustrations here show the different levels required; it will be noticed that plenty of height is needed to carry the linear 2-dimensional framework of the house. If the acting area is low, the design will have to be considered horizontally rather than vertically – perhaps the upper bedroom could rise by three rather than eight steps.

Of course, if rostra and building materials are not available to construct higher levels, the stage floor can be used. Nothing need prevent the ingenuity of the designer from finding a solution!

A composite setting : ground plan for 'Death of a Salesman'

Above: the general setting.

Right: evening, the kitchen area.
Lighting is concentrated downstage centre.

This particular play is most suitably played against and behind gauzes to achieve some of the dream quality required by the author. Funds will not always extend to this, but very well placed lighting for each room can achieve a reasonable substitute for gauzes.

8 Permanent settings – 1: She Stoops to Conquer

Sometimes there is an opportunity to stage a play that will run for a week or longer, giving the designer a chance to try a more expansive or elaborate setting, using a structural framework.

The next few pages show three examples of this type of setting where tubular scaffolding or the newer slotted angle alloy frameworks have been used.

The text of Oliver Goldsmith's 'She Stoops to Conquer' demands a permanent set with two short scenes played before a cloth.

The illustrations and ground plan show a very naturalistic setting with a variety of acting levels.

The major problem for this setting was a lack of headroom in which to roll or 'fly' a cloth for the two short scenes (the Three Pigeons inn and the garden of the house). The solution was to make use of a concertina screen (see page 66 for details) painted on both sides and reversible by means of a simple hooking device.

The ground plan and the lower photograph from the page opposite show the position of the screen when closed and the effect when open for the Three Pigeons scene. (The garden scene is not shown here.)

An example of a working drawing where an elevation is necessary to help those constructing the set to understand the plan view more clearly.

Elevation drawing for 'She Stoops to Conquer'

Ground plan for 'She Stoops to Conquer'

Two scenes from a scale model: Above: Mr. Hardcastle's house – the main setting.

Below: The Three Pigeons – a short scene using mobile screens that are reversible for the garden scene on the back.

The stair arrangement which may at first glance appear complicated was in fact made up of central rostra with three sets of steps arranged round them (more details on page 37 of the section on rostra).

The balcony, constructed with tubular scaffolding, is shown at different stages of construction in the setting on page 99.

The completed set for 'She Stoops to Conquer' is shown overleaf.

She Stoops to Conquer

The close-up photograph below illustrates some of the details in this kind of naturalistic setting. The properties department needs to be rather busy accumulating pieces of furniture as much in the eighteenth-century period as possible. The framed pictures shown here were painted with the setting but many cheap second-hand pictures can be obtained. Some large department stores and antique dealers are prepared to loan reproductions and furniture if given credit in the programmes.

The animal heads are less easy to find but are not essential to the setting. The candle-sticks are battery-operated (their manufacture is described on page 139 of the section on properties). A gun replica may be obtained or the gun be made – see page 223 of the section on arms and armour. The panelling on the walls and fireplace was all painted – see details on page 132 of the section on painting.

Lighting for the play was concentrated at F.O.H. with another group of Fresnel spots on batten No. 1 for the inn and garden scenes – all other lighting was off in order to black out S.L. behind the concertina screen.

Building a permanent setting

The illustrations show the building of rostra staging, steps and balcony for a production of 'She Stoops to Conquer' in a school hall – described on pages 96 and 97.

Above: Two views of tubular scaffolding balcony showing framework and open sides of rostra. See pages 28 and 29 for rostra construction, pages 10 and 11 for types of scaffolding.

Right: The completed carpentry work before putting up the flats and stage front, and before lighting.

Note the hall lights which were later removed and replaced by F.O.H. lighting.

Permanent settings – 2: Twelfth Night

The setting shown on this and the next two pages is permanent only in the sense that the main structures (consisting of central rostra, steps and ramp) remain unchanged from scene to scene. All changes of locality and sense of time are achieved through lighting and properties.

This particular production posed a problem: it was first to be staged on a traditional proscenium stage and later to be transferred to a large hall as an arena production with the audience on three sides. The setting had to allow for the change.

The preliminary sketches on the right show one possible solution to this problem. The set is built up from rostra and steps with a skeletal frame – the steps being quite low and open underneath to avoid obscuring the view from the sides in the arena arrangement. The two sketches also illustrate the ways of using a strong lighting change on a cyclorama – giving a complete reversal of silhouette from dark to light.

Although it may appear to be a very large undertaking to build this set again in new surroundings, the assembly can in fact be done in a matter of four or five hours with a large team of helpers. All fixing has to be carefully planned but it is not too difficult if measurements are accurate and all the jointing sound in construction.

Right: three sketches for Shakespeare's 'Twelfth Night'. Above, with cyclorama lit; centre, with forestage lit; below, with drapes across central arches and general lighting.

The scale model as an independent setting for an arena production.

Twelfth Night

The pictures on this page show how the idea of an adaptable setting was developed from ground plan into scale model. The rostra stage has a sunken area in centre-stage to allow a passageway under the balcony – this creates another acting level. It is always useful to make a number of different levels for Shakespearean productions because of the many scenes. Certain areas can then be turned into small 'insets', e.g. the curtained space under the balcony indicates a separate room.

Ground plan for 'Twelfth Night' - a step and rostra setting with cyclorama

The same scale model as above fitted within the proscenium model theatre.

Three scenes from 'Twelfth Night' – all within the proscenium setting.

Left: with cyclorama and S.R. lighting behind the row of columns. (Compare with the original sketch at the top of page 100.)

With more general centre stage lighting, foliage and urns for the garden settings. (See page 142 for making urns and similar garden properties.)

The lower arches hung with decorated curtains for an interior scene – decorating was done by the batik method described on page 125.

The construction of columns

The two rows of columns (pillars) S.L. and S.R. were made from old cardboard cylinders discarded by paper and textile firms. The columns were linked together by glued scrim and paper and secured on the off-stage side by pieces of slotted angle bolted together. They formed a useful function as wings and helped to create a unity of design with the columns supporting the arches.

The C.S. columns were constructed from stiff paper shaped and glued round a dummy cylinder. When dry, the paper cylinders were removed and fitted round the metal framework supporting the hardboard arches.

Permanent settings – 3: West Side Story

The illustrations on this and the next three pages show scenes from a production of 'West Side Story'. It uses as a basis a semi-permanent setting. The set consists of a permanent construction – in this case, the archway – with various mobile, revolving and inset pieces of scenery to make frequent changes of location. The variety of scenery, with carefully placed and controlled lighting, produces an effective range of mood, place and time.

It is essential when designing sets for musicals to understand the special requirements of dance routines and movement. The cast is usually large and needs to move freely over the stage area.

The designer must offer the maximum in clear stage space and must avoid cluttering up this space with props or other design features during those scenes that require a dance number.

It will be seen from the sketch and ground plan that this production made use of a wide archway over the floor of a hall, giving a clear floor area and a certain sense of claustrophobia and menace appropriate to the location and mood of 'West Side Story'.

First rough sketch.

Ground plan for 'West Side Story'

Two views of the construction of the arch – from above and below.

A view from below: note the wooden spacers which carry the battens. The battens, properly adjusted, form an accurate semi-circle.

West Side Story

The construction of the arch is shown on the left. A slotted angle frame was built from floor level to form a large angular tent across the hall with gangways behind.

Attached to the frame at regular intervals were wooden spacers to carry battens across the depth of the archway.

When the wooden frame was completed large sheets of hardboard were fastened by screws to form a wide semi-circle. The illustrations on the left show a number of sheets in position.

The metal frame.

The wooden frame attached to the metal frame. The radius of the arch is found by using a length of string from a point marked on the floor below the centre of the archway.

Sheets of hardboard screwed to the spaced battens complete the archway. Spaces for exits and small gaps for archway lighting are left open.

The frequent changes of scene (15) and the ten different locations demanded by the synopsis were achieved by the use of large pierced screens drawn across upstage behind the archway, arranged in a variety of ways (see pages 68 and 69 for the construction of this type of screen).

Another device was a mobile structure pivoted centre S.R. ('stage right' when looking towards the audience) to the side of the arch – a large hole being allowed to accommodate its return. This structure served both as the bridal shop interior and as the drugstore.

A balcony downstage right led into an inset within the top front of the archway for the two bedroom scenes – see the illustration on the next page.

The space below the balcony provided limited room for the orchestra – see the ground plan on page 103 for details.

The audience was seated on tiered rostra to assist the view of those at the rear. This type of seating arrangement can be seen on page 7.

Above: under the highway. Holes pierced in the roof of the arch allowed archway lamp lighting through the holes.

Below: the 'neighbourhood'. One screen was used at the back.

105

Above: the bridal shop. The mobile was pulled out from the arch.

Below: bedroom 'inset' scene with the street below.

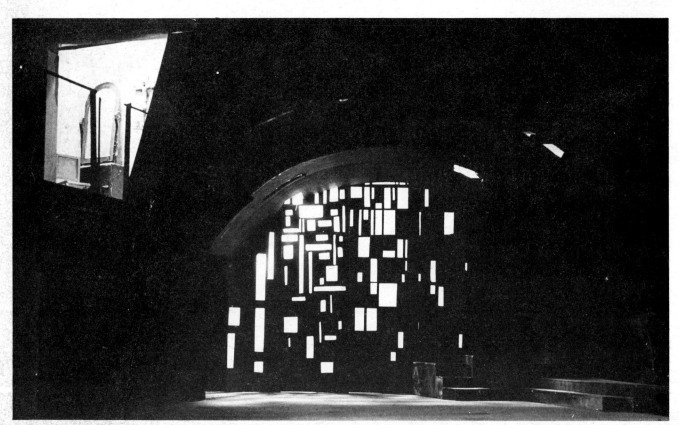

Painting and printing 5

MATERIALS · PREPARATION · 2 AND 3 DIMENSIONAL EFFECTS

THE WORKING SPACE

A large high workshop or hall is the ideal studio for scenic painting. The importance of height is apparent when flats of 3 metres or more need painting side by side to create a unified wall surface.

Some schools and amateur dramatic societies may well lack sufficient space in a workshop but may have free use of the stage for painting purposes. This arrangement can be even more satisfactory with the flats assembled in their correct positions – but ensure that sufficient light is available, whether daylight or general lighting from stage floods or 'house' lighting.

If space is not available, then the flats must be painted in horizontal positions, perhaps flat on the floor or leaning against the wall. The floor position is tiring and trestles or benches will make a good working height.

Ensure that plenty of working top area is at hand for materials, or use a trolley as illustrated below. Note also that water and heating are easily accessible.

Right: a painting trolley can be built or adapted from an old card table with an under-shelf and castors. It will hold most of the necessary materials. It will not, however, be suitable on a raked stage unless castors are omitted or braking blocks are used.

*Below: examples of suitable heating – **a** a gas ring, **b** electric hot-plates and **c** a camping gas stove.*

BRUSHES AND PAINTING AIDS

A wide assortment of good quality paint-brushes is essential for satisfactory scenic painting.

The most useful are:

a a 15–20 cm pure bristle brush for 'laying in' (the covering of large surfaces);

b an assorted range of 25, 50, 75 and 100 mm pure or mixed bristle brushes for finer work;

c small fitches (detail scenery brushes): round, square and cut-angle (cutting-in brushes) – brushes for detailed work and lining (the drawing of lines);

d a paint roller and tray for other kinds of wall painting and printing block techniques;

e sponges and rags for specialised textures;

f a straight-edge for lining, fitted with an old door handle;

g a painter's mahl-stick – useful for resting the arm when painting details on a vertical surface;

h a range of buckets, large tins with handles and other containers for paint – a wire handle inserted through smaller tins can be helpful.

SCENIC COLOUR

The pigment colours are in powder form and are the basic ingredient for all kinds of paint. Added to this pigment is a fixing agent which binds all the particles together. Fixing agents used in scenic painting are 'size', a glue powder that dissolves in hot water, and emulsion glaze.

Available in about sixty colours, the pigments are sold by weight. Although many of the primary and earth colours can be obtained in some decorators' shops and paint shops under the general term of 'decorators' colour' it seems to be increasingly difficult to obtain the variety of colour needed. There may be good stocks in certain places; otherwise it is advisable to order from scenery suppliers – firms are listed on page 276.

All the colours are, of course, intermixable and hundreds of tints and shades can be obtained by selecting from the lists on suppliers' colour cards. For practical purposes only a limited range of colours will be required: whatever colours you choose for a particular production there will be only certain basic colours needed for all scenery.

I have found the following colours the most useful:

White: powdered 'whiting' for general priming and tinting, and pure scenic white for intense colour (usually zinc white).

Black: vegetable 'lamp' black or 'dense' scenery black.

Yellows: lemon – a pale cool yellow,
chrome – a warm strong yellow (mid-colour),
ochre – warm deep earthy yellow.

Reds: crimson – deep cool red,
red ochre – dark red earth,
vermilion – bright orange-red (expensive).

Greens: Brunswick – deep bluish green,
emerald – cool mid-green.

Blues: ultramarine – very deep intense cold blue,
Prussian – a strong blue, tinged with green.

Browns: Raw Umber – a yellow brown,
Raw Sienna – a reddish brown,
Vandyke – very dark.

The primary colours (red, yellow and blue) cannot be made by mixing and are essential for good clear painting. The secondary colours (green, orange and purple) can be made by mixing pairs of primaries. If, however, a bright intense green is required, buy emerald green rather than mixing blue and yellow. Mixing tends to dull colours slightly.

Quantity depends on the area to be covered – but order more than you think you require, especially of whites and blacks which always seem to run uncomfortably low at critical times!

The powder colours are usually sold in paper or polythene bags but should be transferred to more substantial containers. Label clearly and secure with lids for storage.

Dyes and metal colours

Cloths, curtains, transparent gauzes and other fabrics are all textiles that can be dyed. These materials (with certain exceptions to be explained later) are not suitable for general painting and require aniline dye treatment. (Dye is permanent and cannot be washed out.)

Dyes have the advantage of staining the material without the thickening quality of paint and give intense and brilliant surface effects to costume and curtaining.

Available in about 20 colours and sold by weight, they are fixed with a salt known as Glauber Salts. Mixing instructions are available from the suppliers (page 276).

Many new dyeing techniques have been developed. Write to suppliers for information – see page 276.

Metallic colours

Bronze powders are available in a wide range of metallic colours: pale, medium and deep gold and silver, and nickel (a dull silver).

Aluminium powders are sold in greens, purples, blues and reds – these mix well with the bronzes.

All these metal powders can be fixed with 'gold' size (a thin varnish), shellac (glue in methylated spirit), P.V.A. medium and even thickened size water. Each fixative depends on the use. Gold size, shellac and P.V.A. are for properties; thinned P.V.A. for costumes; size water for scenery and some textiles. Experiment on various scrap materials to achieve the desired effect.

Lacquer, enamel and emulsion paint

Where hard brilliant shine is required on furniture or properties, a Chinese lacquer is suitable. Enamel paints can also be used but take longer to dry.

Although relatively expensive compared with a powder colour and size mixture, emulsion paints can be useful for certain scenery work and require no fixing agent. Emulsion is also waterproof and can be painted over without the sullying effect of an under-painting accidentally spoiling the new brushwork. A disadvantage, however, is that repeated painting of scenery cannot be removed as with powder colours.

Paint sprays

All enamel and metallic colours are now available in aerosol tins. Although quick and easy to use, spray painting tends to be indiscriminate and wasteful unless large areas are to be covered. Some interesting effects can be obtained by using paint sprays with stencils.

Fixing Agents

Size powder is obtainable in small or bulk quantities according to need. A half-kilogramme packet will make about 5 litres of size water.

Emulsion glaze is obtainable ready for mixing with powder colours. Unlike size, it requires no heating.

Animal glues in 'pearl' crystals or flake or as a size powder are useful for thickening colours, sticking down card, canvas and paper, adding montage/collage surfaces before painting. (A wide range of adhesives for various needs is listed on pages 273-5.)

Shellac This is glue in methylated spirit which is useful for metallic colours. It is sold in flake or powder form to which methylated spirit must be added. It can also be purchased in liquid form. The clear shellac is the most suitable.

Assorted pigments, powders and liquids used in scenic painting.

PREPARATION: Size . . .

Put 1 part of size into a bucket, add about another part of cold water and allow to soak for a short time.

Pour seven parts of boiling water to make up a bucketful of hot size water, stirring well until completely dissolved.

If large areas of scenery need to be covered in a short time, make up a further bucketful.

Left-over size water can be stored for a short time but must be reheated each time that colour is made up.

. . . and powder colour

Half fill a large bucket with whiting and add cold water just to cover the powder.

Soak and break up any lumps. Leave overnight to allow good blending of the powder and water.

This white will be your basic primer for preparing canvas.

Half fill a smaller bucket with black powder colour if you require dark backings and dark areas for the setting. Again, mix with cold water to a thick paste.

Prepare these and all the other colours you require (by matching as closely as possible the colours on rough sketches or scale models) and mix to a consistency of thick paste.

Mixing size and colour

The proportion of hot size to prepared colour should be about 50 : 50. Pour the size slowly into the colour, stirring all the time. Test the covering capacity of the mixture, taking care not to add too much size water.

To sum up: make all your powders into a paste with cold water and then into a thin cream with hot size.

The covering power (opacity) of colour can be tested by dipping a piece of card into the mixture – if the strength of colour remains and the colour stays fixed, the mixture will be suitable. No under surface should be seen through the paint.

Colour mixing and matching

Select and mix your colours taking care to match the colours to sketches or scale model.

Scenic colours always dry lighter than expected, so prepare your colours accordingly by making each colour a shade or two deeper.

To test the shade of colour, paint an area on a scrap of card or board and hold over heat for a few moments.

Priming

Whether of canvas, board or other material and whether new or old, the surface must first be prepared for painting. (In certain cases an un-primed hardboard can be painted without first priming but this is an exception.)

This preparatory priming coat ('lay-ing in') is applied with the largest brush or roller. If the setting is to be in rather a light colour use the bucket of prepared whiting.

Settings with a strong dominant colour scheme can benefit if the priming coat has some of that colour added – this will make a suitable base for working on.

Avoid overworking the priming coat on old painted canvases or the previous layer of paint will sully the work – quick lively brush work will always give good results. On canvas covered by many layers of paint, wash and scrape off the surface before re-priming.

When dry, test the colour against the scheme required. If too light add more dark mixed pigment, or vice versa.

When satisfied with the mixture, brush outside of container. Liquid colour changes on cooling so headaches will be avoided if you can identify the contents quickly when the colour is next required.

part of scale model

SCALING-UP

To enlarge a scale-model or roughly sketched scene to full size requires a simple scaling-up method. Any detailed work on a backcloth, very large flats or other cloths will require a working method.

If, for example, you make a grid of 1 or 2 cm squares on your 1 : 25 scale model backcloth, you can prepare a grid on a backcloth with 25 cm or 50 cm (0.5 m) squares. The large squares will do for general layout, the 25 cm squares are helpful for any detailed areas.

If you wish to preserve for display purposes sketches or scale model from being marked with grid lines, rule the 1 or 2 cm squares in ink or pencil on tracing paper on top. Mark out the 25 cm or 50 cm lines on the sides of the flat or backcloth. Rub a piece of cord with chalk (for dark backgrounds) or charcoal (for light backgrounds). Hold the cord taut between the marks on the sides of the flats, pull the string away from the surface at the centre and let go with a sharp snap. A clear line should be deposited.

Chalking lines, working across the surface in 50 cm grid lines on large cloths.

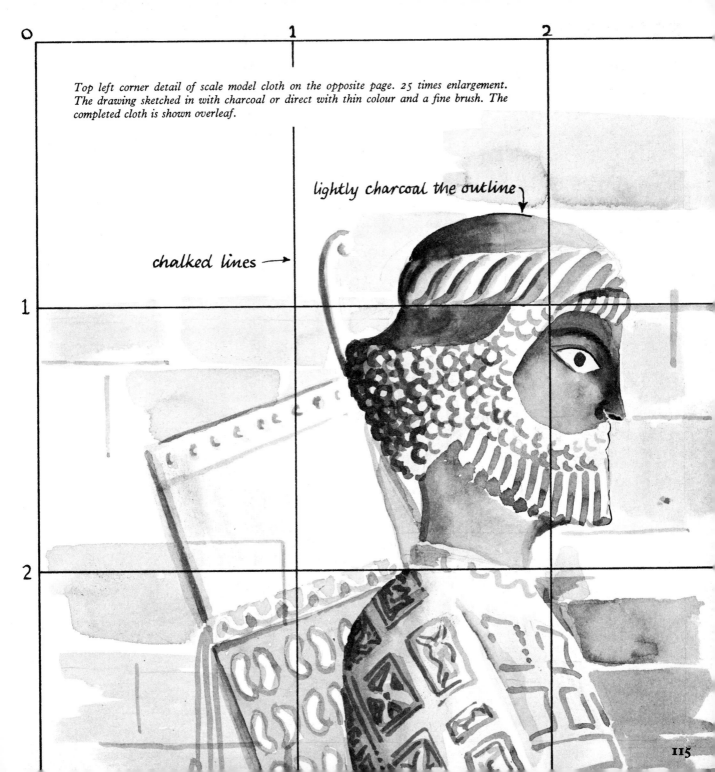

Top left corner detail of scale model cloth on the opposite page. 25 times enlargement. The drawing sketched in with charcoal or direct with thin colour and a fine brush. The completed cloth is shown overleaf.

lightly charcoal the outline

chalked lines →

115

NATURALISTIC PAINTING: Cloths, murals, cut-outs

The Gardens of Babylon scene from 'Adventure Story' by Terence Rattigan. For this scene a realistic backcloth and flats were painted with broad brushes using rather dry colour on the 'bricks'. For the same scene, see also page 166 of the section on properties. Note the canvas cut-out cloth (a 'leg') hanging on the right of the photograph above.

Backcloths (or background cut-outs)

The illustrations on these two pages aim at realism in scenic terms. In the picture above a whole setting is designed to represent an oriental garden. On the facing page the painted 'tapestries' are used more as properties to help evoke a mood in one area only of the stage setting.

Necessary to this realistic approach is research into costume, architecture, painting and sculpture, and also into the social aspects of the period. Research is, of course, needed for all types of design, but here most of all. If particular pieces of sculpture or ceramic are to be represented by painting, the scaling-up method described overleaf can be used in the design. Care should be taken when recreating a mood or place to avoid slavish copying; shape, colour and detail should be selective and simplified.

Remember that form and colour must blend into an overall concept of the play.

Cloth cut-outs

Always paint cut-outs before cutting to avoid curling. Additional layer of canvas or, better, an area of gauze should be glued behind to strengthen and to prevent curling.

Right: Juliet's bedroom from 'Romeo and Juliet' – showing a mural (wall-painting) and some panelling. These transform the 'tomb' part of the setting shown on page 129. The iron gates are replaced by net curtains and the back wall is covered by the mural.

Below left: one of the two mediaeval hunting scenes used as a decorative foil to the walls on either side of the setting for 'Henry IV Part 1' shown on page 84 (the border is done by stencil – see page 122).

Below right: example of a cut-out – showing a rather free and fluid use of the brush.

SURFACE PAINTING

All painted surfaces need a variety of treatment, from simple colour washes to more complex textures.

Look carefully at a 'plain' wall, free of all decoration. At first glance it may appear uniform but a light source falling across it will throw a more intense light on one part and make other parts 'fade' away or perhaps make a shadow.

This awareness of gradations, of tone on flat surfaces, is essential to scenic painting if variety and interest are to be achieved.

So whatever base or background colour, always have one or two colours close in tone and hue for adding to the base colour. These will be helpful in some of the methods described here.

(Definitions of some terms used in painting and design are included in the section on design – pages 72–73.)

Backgrounds

'Grounds' or background colours can be either the priming coat (the 'laying-in' coat mentioned earlier), or a colour wash on top of the primer. Large backcloths, borders and legs can be built up with a large brush or broom using two or three metal trays of related colours – blue, blue/green and emerald, for example – dipping the brush freely from colour to colour or using separate brushes. Atmosphere and mood will be evoked if the brushwork is free in application – avoid too flat an appearance on large areas.

SURFACE TREATMENT

To give interest and variety to any surface (apart from straightforward brushwork), a number of texture techniques can be tried. Four techniques are in frequent use in the theatre:

1 spatter and splash
2 scumbling and drybrush
3 stippling and daubing
4 ragroll and paint roller

Also to be described are methods of patterning a wall or textile, giving the effect of wallpaper or similar surface decoration. These methods fall into four groups:

1 stencils
2 block prints
3 batik printing
4 screen printing

There is also a small section on painting gauzes.

Finally, one can create surfaces that stand out in a third dimension – built up on flats or rostra to achieve a more solid effect. Many traditional materials are used but new materials are also introduced:

1 wood debris – sawdust, chippings and shavings
2 plaster
3 expanded polystyrene sheet of varying thicknesses
4 scrap material; newspaper, metal foil, old canvas, etc.

Each surface will be illustrated in turn.

an alternative position – working on the floor from centre to edges

← trays of related background tones

Painting a cloth or group of flats with two or more related colour tones. Large decorator's brushes or brooms can be used, the colours are contained in wide trays or buckets.

Painted textures – 1

1 Spatter and splash

This is a flicking method with a brush, producing much mess unless the floor and other surfaces are well protected by old newspapers. It is most effective in breaking up a uniform even surface and for producing gradation from light to dark. Using two or more tones of colour on a base colour or other textured surface, a wide variety of effects can be obtained. The paint should be of a creamy consistency.

2 Scumbling and drybrush

With the scumbling method, the brush is 'worried' or twisted about with strong wrist work to produce an uneven swirling surface texture. The paint needs to be slightly thickened. Drybrush painting requires fairly thick colour which is dragged lightly across the surface producing a broken colour with the under-painting revealed below.

Two or more shades of colour will make a richer surface texture.

Both methods are applied with the intention of combining top and under-painting effects.

A scene from 'The Merchant of Venice' showing two of the textures described on this page: the background is dark, the stones are scumbled in and spatter work is applied on some parts over the scumbling.

Spatter – knock against the other arm to produce spray.

Scumbling – active twist to the wrist – not much pressure.

Drybrush – drag lightly across the surface.

Stippling with a large brush. The square flat upstage is stippled in three tones of ochre and yellow. (Scene from 'Julius Caesar').

3 Stippling and daubing

Use an old well-worn bristle brush with fairly dry colour for stippling textures. Dab the brush at the surface to produce a variety of dot or spotted areas. Use different pressures and do not overload the brush with paint – only a small amount is required at a time. A small sponge (with open pores) is also very effective for more concentrated masses.

4 Ragroll

Two techniques can be used with rag textures.

a roll the rag over the wet painted surface to spread and break down the uniformity.

b wrap the rag round a paint roller (it can be secured with string). Apply a fairly creamy paint from paint tray and roll in all directions for a lively and agitated surface, or vertically only for a more restful and calm effect.

The latter effect can make a successful backing for block, screen or stencil work. (See photograph right.)

A close-up of a ragroll used on a wet paint surface.

Above left: ragroll used alone.
Below left: stippling with short, quick dabs.

Roller texture

A paint roller using rather dry colours and applied without too much pressure can be a useful aid to surface treatment. Placed with care it can reproduce a stone wall, both in the scale of actual stones and the roughness of the stone surface. Variations in the size of each stone block can be achieved by careful use of the roller, in direction and in pressure. (See small illustration below.)

Stone blocks – the narrow blocks are produced by turning the roller in a vertical direction.

The rag roller pulls gently down the flat without hurry – the rag will slip if rushed.

A flat with a rag-roll surface looking like patterned fabric.

Note the four roller widths, using a rag-roll in one tone of background texture.

The use of rag wrapped round the roller can be effective for producing an interesting backing to various kinds of overlaid pattern. The illustration on the left shows a vertical rolling technique together with a few drybrush lines. On top there is a block pattern in lighter colour. The method of block printing is described overleaf.

Patterned surfaces

Apart from cost, the use of actual wallpaper for stage interiors is not suitable or desirable – the designs are usually too small and, from a practical point of view, the paper would be difficult to stick to rough canvas or to remove when the flats are required again.

1 Stencils

To simulate a large patterned wall surface the most useful method is the stencil. Make the stencil from prepared waterproof stencil paper; otherwise use stiff paper or thin card and treat the surface with shellac or any quick-drying paint after the pattern has been cut out.

Waterproofing the stencil will avoid the curling of edges. If you have a large area to cover it is advisable to have an extra stencil in reserve as they have to take a lot of rough treatment and can break down with too much use.

To be effective from a distance, the pattern should not be too small. A minimum of 30 cm for the stencil will give a reasonable-sized pattern from the back of the auditorium.

Your design may consist of one, two or even three parts. Cut your stencil on a smooth surface with a sharp knife and make a register mark at the sides and/or at the top and bottom to ensure that the pattern can be repeated successfully. Apply colour by stippling with a short stiff bristle, dipping only lightly into paint and stippling off the surplus on to scrap material – never use much paint on the bristle as it may overflow behind the stencil. Paint running down the canvas (or board) after the stencil has been removed can be very aggravating!

A sponge may be used as an alternative to a bristle. Sprayed paint can also be used but some preliminary attempts should be made and the surface to be printed masked where necessary.

As an alternative to colouring through a cut stencil, a design can be 'pricked' through the stencil with a nail and then pounced through with a charcoal bag. The design is then lightly indicated and may be developed in a freer style with a paint brush. This method is only suitable on smooth surfaces.

A double stencil pattern – two shades of colour on a light ground.

Cutting the stencil – to ensure that no loose pieces drop out leave 'ties' across.

Stippling through stencil – a faint vertical line in charcoal ensures accurate positioning.

2 Block prints

The block illustrated on the left was used over the ragroll surface on page 121.

The printing technique requires pressure to be applied to the printed surface. Most canvas flats are therefore unsuitable for this treatment unless very taut indeed. It is however an interesting method on hard surfaces, such as hardboard, and can make attractive texture patterns on a large scale.

This block and the 'brick' block below were both made from expanded polystyrene sheet of 25 mm and 15 mm thicknesses respectively. The method of making the blocks is as follows:

1 Glue a sheet of hardboard or pin-board to the back of the polystyrene sheet with P.V.A.-based glue. Apply pressure and leave to harden. This will prevent breakage.

2 Paint the design on the polystyrene with thick creamy paint.

3 While still wet, pass the design quickly across a candle flame so that all unpainted parts will shrink back.

4 The block is ready for printing. Roll over the design with thick paint and press firmly down.

If 'realistic' brick walling is required, a very quick and effective method is to combine a block print with brush and spatter work.

Below: seven courses of bricks printed at once! The diagram shows how the block printing slots together. The block was prepared as described above. The slightly broken surface of expanded polystyrene gives realism to the whole wall surface. Spatter on top and mix the shades of colour.

alternate prints – raise or lower block one course

Right: close-up of the block and the printed image – part of the brick arch for 'West Side Story' – see pages 104 and 105.

3 Batik printing

Another way of printing fabrics, offering a much wider variety of texture and colour, is *batik*. A craft originating in Java and Indonesia and now popular the world over, it is ideal for costume and for special concentrated colour spots within a stage setting.

Batik is a form of resist printing, using hot wax. The pattern or image is applied with special tools dipped in the wax and worked over the fabric. The fabric is then dyed – the areas untouched by the wax take the colour. Cold water dyes are used most frequently to prevent the wax from melting. After dyeing the wax is boiled off and the cloth washed and ironed.

Materials and equipment:

A heater – gas ring, electric hotplate, etc.

A form of double boiler – glue pot or tins within a saucepan.

A collection of tins (with holes punched in the sides) that can contain small night-lights or shortened candles – used as miniature heaters when a large group is working in batik.

A non-metallic bowl or bath for dye.

A liquid measure.

Rubber gloves.

Storage and mixing jars.

Plenty of newspapers.

Some plastic spoons.

The most suitable materials for dyeing are cotton, calico and linen.

Candles or blocks of paraffin wax.

Resin or beeswax.

The tools – tjanting for fine lines and dots, brushes for spreading wide areas.

Some of the equipment.

Method of application

Cut up the candles or paraffin wax into small pieces and put into small tins within a saucepan of water. Boil the water over the heater.

If a large group is working distribute hot wax in small individual tins and tin-heaters. Return the wax to the main heater occasionally if it cools off.

A small quantity (approximately 1 : 5) of beeswax or resin will make the wax less brittle and easier to work.

Spread a number of layers of newspaper on a flat surface. Stretch fabric over a frame and pin; alternatively, pin the fabric over the edges of a table, inserting strips of wood all round the top surface of the table to prevent the fabric touching the newspaper and depositing wax on it.

A tjanting.

Pinning the fabric.

wax pattern

The tjanting in use making a linear kind of pattern. See result on curtains (right).

Blocks for batik printing

Blocks for printing quite large patterns can be made from scrap materials: corks, tubes of various sizes, all kinds of scrap metal provided that the printing surface is flat. The 'block' is dipped into a wide tin lid of hot wax and then pressed down firmly on the fabric surface.

The dyes

These must be suitable for cold water application. Ideal for this purpose are Dylon dyes, but many other brand names are available.

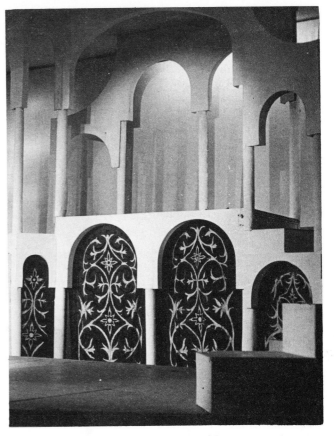

A set of curtains using the batik process – within a stage setting for 'Twelfth Night' (see also page 101 for further scenes of the same production).

Batik blocks: **a** *cork;* **b** *wooden block with pins – only the pins are dipped;* **c** *a plaster mould block (see page 134 on making moulds) – the top must be smoothed to a flat surface;* **d** *a home-made stamp block using a dowel rod for the handle – scrap metal is soldered or nailed to the base;* **e** *cardboard tube;* **f** *balsa wood with a carved base.*

4 Screen printing and dyeing textiles

Curtains, costumes and other soft furnishings (including stage tapestries made from hessian) are best coloured with dye. Scenic paints give a very stiff quality to the material and can crack badly if applied thickly – though they can strengthen the colour effects if used with care.

Aniline dyes are sold in powder or crystal form: the former is dissolved in cold water, the latter in hot. Each needs to be 'fixed' with a salt called Glauber Salts. (See list of suppliers on page 276.)

When a large pattern is required on a textile, the silkscreen technique can be a quick and effective method. Using a panel of silk, cut-out paper stencils and aniline dye mixed with a polycell water paste, an area measuring 10 m × 4 m can be covered within a day. It is an advantage if the textile to be printed has already been dyed – it gives greater colour and textural effect. If the under-dyeing is uneven the overall appearance of the drapes will be enhanced.

Tapestries

Free painting with aniline dyes on hessian stretched over a frame is most effective for stage tapestries. Batik (using hot wax) and tie-and-dye methods can also be effective for large sun-spot backgrounds and costumes. Both techniques – and others – are described in any book about the dyeing of textiles.

1 Use tacks or a staple-gun to fix a piece of silk to a prepared wooden frame.

2 Cut out a paper stencil – the dimensions to fit inside the silk frame.

3 Lay the stencil inside the frame against the silk and seal off all edges with sticky tape. Repeat the whole process for any second colour stencil.

4 Pour liquid dye into the polycell paste and stir well. Prepare a second colour of dye if needed. Use a rubber blade or 'squeegee' of the right width for the frame.

5 Pull squeegee over the stencil using a generous amount of colour. Use downward pressure over all parts of the stencil. (A car window squeegee can be used for small stencils.)

6 Repeat the process with a second stencil or colour if desired.

PAINTING GAUZES

Since it is used primarily for atmospheric effects (see page 24 on the lighting of gauzes) a gauze must retain its transparent quality when coloured. Dyes are the obvious solution as the gauze is then stained and not clogged with paint.

For more 'solid' (opaque) effects, e.g. walls or various silhouettes, thin or thick paint can be dragged across the gauze. Lit obliquely from the front a strong shape or silhouette will stand out, fading only if a light is brought up behind and the front light dimmed out.

Left: detail showing part of a curtain with the screen design described in the diagrams. This design can be seen in a setting on page 93.

Right: a gauze with front lighting only – picture of a woman.

Far right: the same gauze in the workshop with back lighting only.

3-Dimensional surfaces – 1

Many other textural surfaces can be created by means of collage or by building up the surfaces with a variety of materials. Such surfaces have the slight advantage over the painted texture that they will all stand out well with oblique stage lighting over them, giving a strong three-dimensional appearance.

1 WOOD DEBRIS: sawdust, shavings and chippings

Sawdust and other debris can be sprinkled on a glued or thickly sized surface, or mixed with paint before the paint is applied to the surface. The photograph on the right shows the quality of surface achieved by such means.

2 PLASTERING

Layers of plaster are trowelled on to the canvas before painting. Swirled around freely (whiting having been added to the mixture) it is slow-drying and will stand working on for some hours.

This sort of surface can add variety to a large wall. The plaster can have dye added or can be painted over when dry.

Sawdust

Wood chippings

Plaster with finger pattern texture.

Plaster as surface texture – note the oblique lighting.

Wood shavings

A setting using geometrical shapes, with walls covered in expanded polystyrene sheets and areas of paint. (Churchyard scene from 'Romeo and Juliet') A close-up on page 117 shows the inset tomb scene transformed into a bedchamber.

3 EXPANDED POLYSTYRENE

New materials are worth experimenting with in theatre design. One of the most versatile is expanded polystyrene. In massive form it can be sculpted with hot wire (see also page 147 of the section on properties) and in sheet form it can be used as a printing block (page 123) or, as in the illustration above, as a wall surface. (See page 48 for a note on fireproofing.)

In a rather austere design for 'Romeo and Juliet' it was decided to give the walls more of a three-dimensional effect by adding a surface with varying sizes of sheet. The wall behind the plaster and wire crucifix was covered with a mixture of small and medium pieces with a few painted squares. The large tomb entrance at the centre and stage left used much larger tiles and revolved to show further wall coverings (see page 45 for mobile rostra and page 144 for crucifix).

3-Dimensional surfaces – 2

The back wall: a close-up of textures. The tree prop and milestone (rather out of focus) are for a daytime setting – see page 155 for the two props.

Scrap material: newspaper, metal foil, etc.

These two views of a setting for the musical 'Oliver' show a variety of 'solid' texture and illustrate the point that lighting creates a strong feeling of three dimensions.

Newspapers, brown wrapping paper and all papers that fold and crumple easily make a material for these effects. Soak in size water for a few minutes and gently press against old flats or other backings not required for repainting.

Left: a complex of three-dimensional textures – newspaper swinging across the lower part of the wall, pieces of plastic and narrow strips of plywood separating tones into near-vertical sections.

The design intention was to create a mood of seediness and dirt in a poor part of Dickensian London. Some of the mould and pollution associated with dank, moist dockland were also in mind.

Right: a wider view of the same setting with a few changes of props and mobile flats together with a new direction of lighting to create a more sinister mood. The high relief of shadow is well in evidence here.

This setting embodies most of the painted and built-up textures described in this section of the book. Note the two large mobile trucks — see page 43 for their construction.

LINING

Care should be taken in measuring and marking out panelling for an interior set. When sketching or using chalked line as described on page 114 and a plumb line always measure from the stage level and not from tops of flats and cloths – this will ensure equal height throughout a series of flats and rostra. For long walls use the chalked line as described on page 114 and a plumb line for main verticals.

Using one of the fitch liners (10 mm, 15 mm or 20 mm as appropriate) loaded with a highlight colour, run across the straight-edge. Complete all highlights, noting carefully your source of light so that edges of the panelling catch the light correctly.

Repeat the process for the shadow lines. Ensure that you prepare sufficient colour for each shadow line and that shadow lines are all tonally related to the base colour. Where a softened effect is needed to suggest a curved or cylindrical surface, use a clean wet brush to blend the still moist colours together.

A scene showing the technique of lining. The panelling and wood 'relief' together with the moulding on the banister newel posts are all painted. (Scene from 'She Stoops to Conquer' – a more detailed view of the setting is on page 98.)

Blending edges

To avoid an abrupt contrast at the top of flats between the painted surface of the flats and the curtain borders above, soften off the top of the flats by dragging a dry brush dipped in black or another suitable dark colour to match tone of the borders. Start with pressure on the top edge and gently lift the brush away from the surface. This technique can also be used on vertical edges where a similar softening is required. (See the setting for 'Bernadette' on pages 90–91 as an example.)

Properties 6

LIGHTING PROPS · SCULPTURE · THRONES
· OUTDOOR PROPS · FOOD AND DRINK

THE WORKING AREA

Reasonable facilities for working are required for the making of properties. Some items, such as small goblets, require little space, whereas a large throne needs considerably more.

Conditions for working will obviously vary from place to place but an ordered arrangement should always be the aim, whether in a cramped classroom or the ideal workshop.

Each differing process of manufacture requires a clearly defined working area, especially where large groups of people are working as teams. One should aim at three or four areas at least.

If, for example, paper pulp is being used at the same time as varnish, shellac glue and enamel paint, try to avoid any overlapping in the use of the materials. Then the likelihood of spoiling a well-prepared 'prop' can be eliminated.

Another essential for smooth progress at all stages of manufacture is good storage.

The storage area needs plenty of cupboard and shelf space with all necessary items well labelled and, if possible, arranged in well defined groups. *Adhesives* will include every type of glue, contact adhesives and sticky tapes; *fastening and fixing* all screws, nails, tacks, staples, etc. *Containers* are well worth collecting: metal tins from tobacco to biscuit size are the most useful (especially the smaller ones); many kinds of plastic pots and small buckets, often with clip-on lids – handy for liquids and glues and also for mixing paint.

Always carry a large stock of newspapers and rags. Newsprint is still the most versatile of materials: it can be used for cleaning, protecting working surfaces and making pulp and mâché.

THE MATERIALS

A complete list of necessary tools and materials is shown on pages 274 and 275. Not all are essential and certain items will seldom be required. It is only necessary to experiment to discover what is most suitable for one's needs. However, mention should be made here of one important source of materials – the scrap yard.

Collect scrap of all kinds: factories produce a vast amount of industrial waste and the retail trade discards many kinds of containers. A request to almost any retailer to save certain kinds of refuse will bring many useful items. The author has frequently made great savings on expanded polystyrene, cardboard, hardboard, string, wire, metal foil and scrap sheet metal by such means – thus reserving funds for more durable and expensive items, such as a new spotlight or flood.

Galvanised wire and wire mesh are, with wood, the most essential materials for property making. Keep a stock of thick, medium, and thin wire for the various structures. If space allows, keep a few tea-chests in a back room, cellar or under a bench to store scrap. If each chest is reserved for particular types of thing (plastic containers, tubes and rolls, string and wire, etc.) a large, comprehensive and accessible supply will soon be available.

Occasionally, a new way of making a prop will be suggested by the shape of a scrap item.

Cardboard is always a useful and versatile material for props. The stiff, firm card used in the footwear and clothing trades for containers is excellent. Corrugated card is used in industry for packing purposes: it is pliable and ideal for many curved surfaces.

Note: most of the props illustrated by photographs in this and other sections were constructed and painted by schoolchildren.

Wire and wire mesh

To avoid cluttering the illustrations with excessive labelling in this section, galvanised plain wire and galvanised wire netting (known also as chicken wire) are simplified to 'wire' and 'wire mesh' respectively.

When purchasing these items the correct description for heavy, medium and fine wire is 10 gauge, 12 gauge and 16 gauge galvanised plain wire (note that the higher the number, the finer the wire).

Large, medium and fine wire mesh is sold as galvanised wire netting 25 mm, 18 mm and 13 mm respectively (the measurement refers to the hole size).

LAMPS AND LANTERNS

Lights on stage, such as standard lamps or table lamps, are readily available on hire – or on loan from members of the cast.

Antique lamps, street lamps and fires can be built up from thin wood strip, papier mâché, wire and tissue. The illumination of the smaller lights (hand lanterns, torches) can be achieved by using $4\frac{1}{2}$ volt batteries and torch bulbs, controlled either by switch or by turning the bulb gently in its socket. In the case of candles, the bulbs can be lightly glued and covered with tissue torn to a flame shape – giving quite a realistic effect when lit.

Larger street lamps can be effectively lit by 40 or 60 watt bulbs controlled from the switchboard – the number of tissue layers used will determine the amount of light visible. Old, dirty glass can be effectively suggested by layers of varnish.

17th century pendant lamp

6 cutouts of thick card – tape to thick wire frame above – glue and tack to plywood hexagon

white tissue reinforced with fine muslin – glue lightly to dowels and varnish

scrolls of card and medium gauge wire taped to retain shape – join with tape & wire

chain

lighting flex

paper pulp knob

plywood drilled to take dowelling

25×25 mm wood support

paper pulp

handle – card taped between wires

wire frame

staple

dowel

wire catch

thin plywood support

battery and bulb holder

card shapes taped between wires

plywood top and base

tissue & muslin (see above)

hinge door with tape

Hand lanterns

old thin metal cup or papier mâché

wire hinge for door

wood disc base

wire frame

body of papier mâché on wire frame – or use old metal ashtray

push-button switch

lamp – cover in tissue

battery

heavy gauge wire frame wired and taped to body

paper pulp ornaments

wooden disc for base

Antique lamp

135

Street lamps

Constructed over a rigid wooden support the lamps are given shape and character with various materials. Use wire, wood strips and stiffened felt for frames, varnished tissue or muslin for glass. Paint to simulate weathered look.

50×50 mm softwood post

wire frame
globe of varnished tissues built over balloon

25×25 mm softwood
50×50 mm softwood

felt details

American street lamp

Two street lamps. Part of a scene from 'Oliver' – see also pages 130–31.

Riverside lamp

paper pulp details

card roll

Wall lamp

varnished tissues on inside frame reinforced with butter muslin

25×25 mm softwood

card or felt

papier mâché dolphin over wire mesh built around a 50×50 mm post – can be mounted on a balustrade or be a free standing prop, with extra base height

old lamp shade or papier mâché

metal angle brackets

light flex

plug and socket to separate parts if desired

dowels

heavy gauge wire frame

50×25 mm. frame

globe-tissues and paste built over large balloon

hardboard or plywood cutouts

50×50 mm post

plywood sides

brace on wide base

Lamp post

136

Torches, fires and braziers

For the effect of a live fire, use two lamps. The orange one should be permanently lit, the other orange (or red) one should have a broken circuit using a neon starter switch.

Log fire

- plywood backing
- table tennis balls as knobs
- actual & painted logs on canvas
- turned wood bars
- curved sides of hardboard (can be omitted)
- neon starter (produces flicker)
- tapered legs from 50×50 mm softwood

- 25×25 mm softwood frame glued & screwed
- 50 mm square

Flaming torch

- yellow and orange tissues – lightly oil or varnish to make semi-transparent
- rolled card cone
- felt ring
- paper pulp feet
- electric torch – switch connected to outer casing

- wire and pulp fixings
- rings – heavy gauge wire
- thick card cone – glued and wired
- paper pulp ornaments
- coloured 'gels' or/and tissues lamp
- light flex
- wire or cord bracing
- 3 iron bars for tripod

Brazier

soaked hardboard strips frame – tie together with wire, canvas or tissues

Antique tripod

Above: an antique tripod (the temple fire for sacrificial offerings or, on other occasions, a washing bowl). The small inset shows a brazier with hot coals. Use assorted layers of warm-coloured tissues with one or two lamps—see fires, top left.

137

A great state candelabrum

This page shows a candle-holder large enough for use as a set piece or, in a pair, suitable for flanking the entrance to a royal apartment.

The example shown consists of a wire frame secured to a wooden dowel support and a heavy base plate. (For the method of taping wires, see the making of spectacles on page 233.)

total height   2 metres

tack and tape scrolls to discs

central dowel concealed by arm, body and leg of figure

staple wire at closest points to dowel

medium gauge wire framework

fine wire mesh

Figure construction

papier mâché – shellac and paint

tape wires together

card or stiffened felt on wire frame

4 card cutouts

plug and socket

plywood bases

Candle

fire-proofed white muslin

flame or candle lamp

lamp holder

top of 2 metre length of thick dowel

thick cartridge paper or roll for candle

small wood or layered paper ring supports candle

wood disc

50 x 50 mm softwood

Alternative bases

ornamental parts built up in paper pulp, mâché, felt & cord

paper roll for column papier mâché cord / felt

25 mm dowel nail or screw

heads and feet wire mesh, paper pulp or mâché

Candlesticks

mains lighting for candles if required

fine nylon cord

4 ~ or more ~ branches in heavy gauge wire

felt/card screws

A chandelier

spike for large candle ~ or fit battery or mains candle as shown below

wire frame ~ card or felt strips for thickness

Renaissance candle wall bracket

tie wires to wood discs

hollow candle ~ wood ring to secure over dowel

candle paper rolled round dowel and glued

simplified stick ~ dowel with slot sawn out for wires ~ paper pulp/string mouldings

plywood discs ~ hole to fit dowel and turned stick

tack & glue

sufficient space for size of battery

white tissue pasted around bulbs ~ wires soldered to bulb paper disc & rim

hollow paper candle ~ glue or plaster wax drops

all turned wood parts

electric wires round medium gauge wire arms

string ~ soak and shape and glue into decoration required

convex shaping in paper pulp

base parts assembled thus

2 holes for wires

centre drilled for electric wires

A

B

press switch

battery

Single candlesticks

Two methods of building a candlestick: left – using a piece of dowel rod, all mouldings built up with glue and pulp or plastic wood; right – a lathe-turned candlestick (if the height is 25–35 cm it can be turned in one piece – larger ones should be made in parts as shown, to facilitate drilling through centres).

Two-branch Georgian candlestick

(properties in a scene from 'She Stoops to Conquer' – page 98)

Decorative features are built up with papier mâché, pulp and string. The under-painting is black, the finish silver.

139

MONUMENTAL SCULPTURE – 1

Portrait busts, temple sculpture, etc.

Certain plays, usually historical, require large sculptural properties. Some can be painted on to a cloth. If time and labour resources allow, however, a three-dimensional sculpture is worth attempting. The examples on the next few pages give a variety of type and construction methods. (See page 48 for a note on fireproofing expanded polystyrene.)

heavy gauge wire or lead piping

50×50 mm soft wood frame

plywood base

wreath of sized felt

papier mâché over plaster and scrim

sculptural relief built up with paper pulp or plaster

drapes – use scrim dipped in plaster

Scene from 'Adventure Story' – the Temple of Apollo, Delphi. Construction method shown on right.

plywood or hardboard cut-out

structural members in 18mm board or 25mm. polystyrene

either: 1- muslin or scrim dipped in plaster 2- thick brown paper, well sized

wire or string ties

large sheets of newsprint or brown paper glued over scrim/muslin — paint all areas as weathered stone

WREATH

polystyrene or thick card for laurel wreath

HAIR glued, screwed & twisted newsprint

where appropriate large, thin polystyrene sheeting can be moulded to structure in place of paper and scrim - secure with thin wire or string

some drapes can be simulated by scrim dipped in plaster

supports to vertical structural members

25mm thick softwood base

tracks of 25×25 mm. softwood or slotted metal angle

Wood braces

large castors

141

MONUMENTAL SCULPTURE – 2

Garden and street objects

depth of relief dependant on viewpoint and lighting ~ increase depth if seen partly from the side

wire mesh or hessian scrim in plaster for bowls

screwed up newspaper glued to cutout to make body in relief ~ finish with butter muslin and papier mâché

hardboard or plywood cutout

papier mâché

100 × 25 cm softwood

polystyrene segments for lightness

hardboard edge

Street fountain in relief

Urn

Left: garden urn.

Two photographs showing construction and completed urn. Note the use of wire mesh round the wood frame before applying papier mâché. The 'swag' shapes are made by dipping hessian scrim into plaster. See page 102 for urns in a garden setting.

Right: small stone figures.

This stone figure, suitable for fountains or classical garden settings, is constructed with a wood frame, wire mesh and plaster.

The fountain, whose construction is shown on the left, as it appeared in a scene from 'The Merchant of Venice' – other scenes are shown on pages 92–93.

hardboard strips built around a large hoop and supported at centre by 50×50mm softwood post

felt edging for roundels and arches

hardboard arches

cornices and all projections in 75 or 100 × 25 mm softwood planking

plywood or hardboard facing throughout

cardboard roll or other available materials

base of columns in felt, card etc.

rostra base

Market place drinking fountain

Occasionally a market place, courtyard or garden scene can be enhanced by a major property in the central area of the stage. The drinking fountain shown above is built with three sides, if set square to the setting line. Only two sides need be completed if set at 45 degrees.

An octagonal step fountain is shown below with a stone figure, suit able for a courtyard scene. An arcaded backing with or without rostra steps would make a suitable acting area.

figures constructed as described on previous page

bowl shape built up as cupola above right – or an inverted refuse bin lid could be utilised

50×50 mm post

brace

50×25 mm framework – hardboard or plywood sides – top 150×25 softwood

2 octagonal rostra

Garden fountain

courtyard arcade – flats or built up in hardboard on 50×25 mm frame

Architectural detail and structure

200 × 25 mm softwood

fine wire mesh

screwed 25 × 25 mm softwood frame

large nails

Crucifix

Left: crucifix constructed with a wood frame and wire mesh. The modelling can be built up with scrim dipped in plaster for a small crucifix. Any large example would be built up with papier mâché because of weight problems – see page 129 ('Romeo and Juliet').

Below: tympanum. Medieval doorways, especially to churches and chapels, can be enhanced by a sculptured tympanum above. Built over a prepared wooden former, strengthened with galvanised wire, the modelling can be done with wire mesh and finished with papier mâché. If on a small scale, the whole tympanum could be modelled in expanded polystyrene sheet (approximately 3 cm thick) cut with a hot wire – see page 147.

Tympanum over doorways

fine wire mesh

cut felt for shapes at rear of figures

alternative to figures – felt shapes, cut and glued inside frame

deep plywood side and inner curve

medium wire frame-work

papier mâché or plaster and scrim over wire mesh on figures. alternative – use expanded polystyrene weathered stone finish

thin ply-wood

Decorative tympanum

9 plywood sections

Corinthian capital – top shape in plywood, wire frame, sized felt details

plywood side

150 × 25 mm softwood

cardboard rolls for columns →

alternative door – painted planking on board – cut felt scroll work

plywood or composition board base

wood strips

hardboard/plywood top shapes

capitals and bases of hardboard and cut felt

100×25 mm plank

50×50 mm softwood

plywood

paper glued on and fluting painted

tack

tube or cord

thin aluminium alloy sheet

Moulded doors and pillared frame

Ionic capital – heavy gauge wire, staple to frame

plywood square

4 thick felt shapes glued to wire frame

string details

4 plywood discs

25 × 25 mm softwood frame

medium wire mesh – avoid crushing roll

staple to frame

brown or thick paper-paint fluting

assorted plastic or rubber tubing base (wire inside – tie at rear)

Ionic column

Some comparative capitals

Egyptian

felt banded column

Doric

fluted column

Ionic

Corinthian

plain column

Columns can be constructed as shown or be simply assembled by using cardboard rolls – see page 102 for details.

145

SCULPTURAL RELIEFS

Sun motif

Large low reliefs finished in metallic paints or foils can make very effective backings to history plays. Imagine the set of three flats on page 57, with sculptured metallic reliefs under well-placed lighting, as a set-piece for a small hall.

The simple motif illustrated here could also be made from cardboard layers or papier mâché.

cut out motif layers from 25mm expanded polystyrene sheet – use very sharp knife on cutting board

paint and/or spray in metallic colours

cutout polystyrene shapes

metal foil can be glued with P.V.C adhesive to shape

sheet of aluminum alloy plywood or hardboard

frame

The finished relief, constructed as shown on the right. Finish in varying layers of metallic paper, foil and paint.

symbols without a backing can be made from felt cutouts and glued to flats or panels

a

b

battery or transformer

a ~ burning out trophy by moving quickly across flame ~ painted areas resist heat
b ~ using an electric wire cutter ~ both methods use 25 mm expanded polystyrene

Trophies, symbols and architectural frieze

An alternative to painted decoration and ornaments on architectural scenery and properties is 3-dimensional relief. Reliefs are useful for architectural features such as pilasters to which lighting will give a feeling of added depth.

rectangular trophy using polystyrene on backing of plywood or hardboard

symbol in felt or polystyrene on a roundel of plywood

cut felt symbol

festoon ~ or 'swag' ~ of cut felt

old canvas, sacking, as strengthening

brown paper, scrap material, polystyrene sheeting etc. for rocky face.

rock constructed as below

cutout edges to flats

ROCKS

Rocks, or any irregular structure on which people are to stand, will require care in construction. The timber framework and planking should be securely glued and screwed before covering with canvas, felt or stiff paper. Stiffen fabric with shellac or size.

75 × 15 mm softwood framework

50 × 50 mm posts

25 mm thick baseboard ~ saw cut out shape

softwood planking, blockboard or plywood

wire mesh will strengthen large rocks

papier mâché, old canvas or thick brown paper or felt

Low relief ground-row

If only a shallow rock or irregular piece of landscape is required, it can be built as a ground-row in low relief. A narrow ledge can be constructed if necessary.

French brace

plywood cutout

low relief of papier mâché on wire or scrim

side elevation

front elevation

RAILINGS AND BALUSTRADES

Exterior settings occasionally need dividing with walls or railings. Classical exteriors need balustrades and country scenes a fence. A narrow, shallow stage can be given a new sense of depth by these means.

25×25 mm softwood frame-glue and screw

100×25 mm base

Iron railings

paper pulp or old knob from drawer

card

tape

felt

glued and taped card scrollwork →

variations for railing spikes

plywood cutout for backings

French brace

lathe turned

2 or 3 strips of thick felt glued and spiralled round cylinder

plywood or hard board adds thickness

thick bands of felt glued to cardboard cylinder

50×50 mm. softwood screwed to top and base

Stone balustrades

75×25 mm. softwood frame

hinged to allow change of angle and easy storage

French brace

Fencing

This style of fencing appears in a setting for 'Fiddler on the Roof' shown on page 70.

glue and tack hardboard or plywood off-cuts

THRONES

Thrones are among those items of furniture difficult to hire, and yet they are essential to many historical plays.

They will have to be made in the workshop and should be strongly constructed. The easiest method is to build over a stool or the seat of an old chair.

The larger thrones will have to be constructed with wood and board as illustrated on the next few pages.

top of plywood or hardboard

curve of thick card, pinned to side of stool then glued and taped to top

stool or old chair with back removed

plywood cutout

plywood or blockboard top

softwood frame

hardboard sides and front

hardboard edging to simulate thickness plywood backing and sides

shallow rostrum

100 x 25 mm softwood framework in thin plywood or hardboard front and sides

side elevation

2 shallow rostra for steps

Pilate's throne

A simple structure suitable for a primary school Passion play (see pages 240–242 for other Passion play items).

Simple thrones

Basic box shapes with a plinth underneath or a step in front to give importance to the seat.

The Snow Queen's throne

Shapes such as this are related to the fantastic and fairy tale. The throne shown above was designed for a primary school production of 'The Snow Queen' based on Hans Andersen's tale.

decorations of cut felt, string or cord

paint in metallic colours for gold

feet of paper pulp

← alternative design for feet

Throne with footstool

(Egyptian/Oriental with variations in decorations)
Thrones can be elaborate and in two or more sections for the convenience of scene-changers. Traditional wood joints give very strong structure but glued butt-jointing with screws is quite adequate.

100 × 25 mm softwood – mortice and tenon joints

knobs–paper pulp on wire

hardboard

cut felt decorations

blockboard or plywood

hardboard curve tacked and glued

plywood or hardboard cutouts for projections of animal reliefs (footstool used as separate item)

expanded polystyrene decorations

plywood or blockboard

front panel thin plywood

animals cutouts in polystyrene or papier mâché

50 or 25 × 25 mm framework

100 × 25 mm softwood framework

large dowel or 50 × 50 mm softwood

151

Gothic throne

A shape more suitable for the Gothic period. Knobs, pinnacles and a lancet-shaped back can be varied to suit various settings. (See page 84 for an illustration of a throne in its setting.)

ornaments~ bottle tops or paper pulp

two 75 mm wide softwood lengths - cut angles to match backing

wood blocks support curved arms

plywood or hardboard panels

thin plywood or hardboard backing

turned knobs ~ or disused table tennis balls, paper pulp and other scrap

2 lengths of 75 mm wide softwood ~glue and screw

wood strip or sized felt mouldings

heraldic devices ~ stencil, paint or cut felt.

75 mm softwood

build up skirting with softwood~mitre corners

plywood backing

arm sides - either one piece or in two parts for conversion to bench

blockboard or thick plywood ~angled top

plywood cutouts

arcaded central support - butt or tenon joints

cut felt or painted

rectangular shape as alternative to angled type

A double throne or bench

With the addition of a back, this type of bench can be converted into a throne – the same method could be applied to a narrow bench.

hardboard or thin plywood panels and cutouts

100 or 75 x 25 mm softwood frame

hardboard or plywood

secure front panel to wood blocks

paper pulp ornaments glued to front faces ~ see page 235 for method of manufacture

polystyrene cutout panels on front and back ~ protect with sized muslin worked carefully into details

hardboard or thin plywood back

75 x 25 mm seat support and front sides

plywood or hardboard front panel

blockboard or thick plywood seat and sides ~ butt joints and screws throughout ~ or mortice & tenon if preferred

Throne with canopy

A design giving more prominence to the throne; in this example for the court scene from 'The Merchant of Venice' (page 93). Also suitable for the Renaissance period. Built by 14 year old boys.

153

STREET FURNITURE (see page 136 for street lights)

Objects of basically cylindrical form:

shaped card

card shaped to flat cone

tape

POST OFFICE

VR

a – glued cord
b – sized felt
c – thin wood strips felt top and base

old refuse bin lid as alternative
8 hardboard segments

thick card
paper, scrim or chicken wire

finish in papier mâché

hardboard or plywood on wood frame

↖ Victorian pillar boxes

Fire hydrant
(American street)

See also the photograph of a setting for 'West Side Story' on page 105.

card strips glue and tack

25 × 25 mm softwood

thick card or 3 mm plywood

plywood or blockboard

scrap or pulp
tin can (small)
tin lid or wood
plaster and scrim or paper

papier mâché

tin lid
tin can

screw plate to upright

wood pieces to give width to base

Pillar/post boxes

edge with felt

ER

3 plywood discs

cut out slot

3 mm plywood or thick card

25 × 25 mm softwood

foam rubber or plastic gives width to lower part (wood blocks as alternative – see pump opposite)

3 mm plywood or thick card or hardboard

base for stability →

old plastic ball papier mâché

large cardboard cylinder

8 thin plywood sides – taper slightly

paper pulp knob

dowel

rope

thick card

rope

wood blocks

Bollards

hardboard or thick card
plywood discs

thin dowel set
in wood block

25×25 mm
softwood

Capstans

cardboard
cylinder

thick cord

wood disc ~ glue and
nail to secure cylinder

tin alloy sheeting can be
used as alternative to
hardboard on most of
these properties

soak in water
to take curve

To
London
150 M

basic structure
for this type of prop
~varying thicknesses

Milestones & tombstones

50mm thick
~aids stability
~or attach plinth

Village pumps

scrap or paper pulp knob
glued and pin shaped
card~4 pieces

wood block

plywood top

cord and curved
card moulding

rubber/plastic
hose as handle
~wire inside

dowel

metal or
plastic bend

cord
rim

plank
of soft-
wood

glued
cord

card

Signpost

BUTAN 13

STOW 5

BAFORD 12

arms pass
through
slot in post

50×50 mm ~
approx 3 metres
in height

25×25 mm
softwood rails

card

wire
staple

staple wire to
rail and attach
card strips with
glued muslin
~paint to match
rails

tack and glue
card strips

**Frame for
sapling**

plywood disc

construct as fire
hydrant (see
opposite page)

cut felt as
decorative mouldings
or strip polystyrene
~pattern by heat
process (see
page 123)

brace

3mm
plywood
or hard-
board

wood blocks
to widen base

plywood
or blockboard

large base
for stability

155

TREES AND SHRUBS

top edge concealed behind border

The two examples on this page properly belong to the section on flats, but are illustrated here to show the fixture of foliage to the main structure.

joints

wire mesh stapled to cutout

leaves/flowers wired on

braces inside shrub

paint background to match leaves

felt or paper leaves

staples

taped wires

3-dimensional shrub

hardboard or 3 or 4mm plywood cutout

plywood cutout

50 × 25mm frame

Rear view of cut-out tree

French brace

wires for leaves nailed or stapled at rear

25mm plywood or board base

Shrub – a 'set piece' or short ground-row

FLOWERS AND LEAVES

50×25 mm softwood frame

3 wood discs cut out to screw in vertical frame

paper knots twist and glue

bark-screwed newspaper or felt-soak in thin glue

wire mesh

brown paper or thick paper

metal or wood bracing

3-dimensional tree

25 mm board or plywood

When complete, paint with scenic colours.

glue wires between folded paper-glue and cut out shapes

coloured tissue papers for flowers (use related colours)

Grasses

felt or paper

tape

wire

Roses

red, orange

crinkle discs and tape to wire

orange wrapped around red

fold over edges-especially towards the outer edges

25 mm board

75×25 mm or 50×50 mm framework

Tree stump

felt or screwed paper on under-layer of paper

FRAMES

A frame of any shape or complexity to suit a historical period can be made from expanded polystyrene sheeting or papier mâché on a wood base or, if preferred, various scrap items glued to a wood frame.

shape out with electric wire cutter

foil
plywood base
expanded polystyrene 25 mm. thick

wood strip moulding - the top shaped from plywood or layered hardboard

mortice & tenon joints

shape feet from 75×50 mm. softwood

Full-length swing mirror

Miniatures

cardboard bases - frames of card with cord and felt trimmings - paint as wood and gilt.

old cupboard or drawer knobs if available - or paper pulp built on long screws.

cutout in polystyrene or build up with stiffened felt.

Mirror or picture

gilded decoration on papier mâché moulding - hardboard base

heavy gauge wire - wrap and shape with sized felt staple wire

blockboard with felt edging

Dressing mirror on stand

carefully smooth out metal foil over P.V.C. adhesive

'MIRROR'

work from centre towards sides

CLOCKS

Adapting modern timepieces to an antique body:

Left to right: rococo wall clock, Regency bracket clock, 18th century French mantel clock, 1920s' 'Deco' clock.

Nineteenth century clock

glue card sides to wood block

typical modern clock

wood blocks for feet

wood block – height determined by type of clock

opening to fit size of clock face

paper pulp animal head

wire split pin attached to small curtain ring

plywood front

thick card glued and pinned

assorted washers, nuts & knobs on metal rod or thin dowel

old cycle or door bell

shaped metal strips

plywood, metal or plastic sheet

painted face on cut card or old time piece

modern clock behind if desired

assorted metal scrap glued and painted

1700 lantern clock

hardboard curve

REAR CLOCK FACE

sized felt edging

Long case or grandfather

lacquer decoration in Chinese style

150 x 19 mm softwood sides

hardboard or 4mm plywood facing

curved moulding in thick card

50 x 25 mm all horizontal members

16mm beading or felt strips

assorted widths of softwood

159

DRINKING VESSELS: Pots and goblets

A variety of types and construction methods are shown, all using easily obtainable materials. Practically any cylindrical container can be adapted to make a goblet – the plastic containers for yoghourt, cream, etc. are ideal for small vessels (use a P.V.A. or polystyrene adhesive for plastics). All vessels can be made waterproof by a generous coat of varnish inside.

cup – papier-mâché, coconut half or similar shape

equal spaced vertical cuts in cardboard

dowel

screw tin lid to dowel

Some of the drinking vessels illustrated in this section.

plastic cups, tubs, old cycle bells coconuts, etc.

yog

model car tyres for knobs on stems

dowels

wire

cotton reels

metal foils

tin lids

assorted string and cord

felt

thick cartridge paper

cardboard

Collect a wide range of card, cord and assorted scrap materials.

1

glue prepared card as shown – tape stem part to secure

2

application of 3 or 4 layers of papier mâché – use fine sandpaper when dry for smooth finish.

Paste

brown sticky tape to help secure tabs and fill gaps between tabs

3

splay ends

spiral 3 or 4 cords round goblet – glue firmly down

glue/paste tissue paper – work around shape to make cord stand out

← cord rim

4

jewels – thick felt base, pulp or shaped button centre covered with coloured metal foils or lacquers – wine gums can be used as alternative

P V C ADHESIVE

if silver/pewter goblet use dark grey undercoat – umber for golds – mix metallic powders with clear shellac

Cone-shaped chalice

card this shape

thick felt shapes - glue firmly

paper pulp or cord as alternative to felt knobs

build up slope in paper pulp

glue and tape edge to dowel

felt glued to dowel

dowel

tin lid screwed to centre of dowel

Lathe-turned goblet

thick felt decorations

Cylindrical goblet

felt decorations

paper pulp base

knitting needle

glue and tack all cards to wooden discs

glue reels together

cotton reels

saw off end when assembled

2 wooden discs - drill hole same diameter as knitting needle

template for use with lathe if a set of identical stems is required

turned stem

plywood disc

card tacked and glued to base

plywood disc

heavy gauge
wire frame

card and
wire handle
taped

thick
card

tape wire to body

felt edging
top and base

plywood disc

Tankard

Lidded beer tankard

string

string or cord

pulp or metal
oddments

group of tin lids
bolted together

wood/metal handle

cut tin~bolt
to inside tin

split pins
(or screws)

carve
handle or
utilise old
handle

cocoa/bean tin

slightly larger
tin lid~bolt
through tin can

To give a metallic finish, underpaint all vessels with greys/
blacks for silver and pewter; warm browns/umbers for
golds. Finish with two coats of clear shellac.

thick card –
glue edges
firmly and
staple and/or
tape together

glue and tape
cone~shaped
base to main
body

thick felt decorations

Roman tankard

JUGS AND PITCHERS

If liquid is to be used, all surfaces should be varnished thoroughly.

Direct papier mâché method

Papier mâché can be built up over a greased vessel, allowed to dry, cut in half to remove the vessel and re-joined with sticky tape and a final layer of paper. See page 264 for the technique of papier mâché.

cover original vase with pieces of tissue over greased surface

apply 6 or 7 layers of papier mâché and allow to dry →

(if alternating layers are colour dyed each layer can be clearly seen)

using a sharp knife, cut lightly through opposite sides of vase and trim top and bottom edges

gently prise apart both halves and paste down loose ends

reassemble two halves, joining with adhesive tape

glue narrow strip of butter muslin or finger bandage along joins

finish with 2 final layers of papier mâché - allow to dry and lightly sandpaper

wood disc or card base

Concealed-glass method

Large containers for liquid can be built round an existing jar or flagon-type bottle. Simply attach a wire frame for a handle and a spout; then paste paper over the surface area. The card and glue for making the spout must be waterproof. Secure firmly to the top of the jar.

spout glued in position

for jugs cut card spout - glue with P.V.C adhesive - coat with 2 layers of varnish

medium gauge wire frame to secure handle

original vase →

thick card glue to vase will widen base area if required

handle of card or felt & heavy gauge wire

felt rim if required

tape

wood disc base

3 or 4 layers of papier mâché

wires round vase tightened with pliers to secure handle

glued scrim or muslin holds wire firmly

glue trimmings and base with muslin and paper

medium gauge wire frame
joined with adhesive tape

tape card between wires

pass handle wires through wood discs and staple to dowel

size of dowel and wood discs dependant on the scale of jug, pitcher or vase

fine wire mesh

7 layers of papier mâché

cord

staples

shellac all parts before and after painting

lower ring

top rim   spout

methods of taping wires

Wire mesh method

A further method is to make up a wire frame to your own design, based perhaps on a historical shape (see the outlines on the opposite page) and build up the surface with papier mâché. This is not practical if liquid is to be used – only for decorative purposes.

Another useful idea for creating an impression of pottery or porcelain: find a flagon-type cider bottle or some similar large glass bottle, pour paint into it, shake well and pour out the surplus. The effect from a distance will be of glistening porcelain. Mixtures of paint will produce marbling.

Greek   Roman

Italian Renaissance

medieval

Egyptian

Some basic shapes

MUSICAL INSTRUMENTS – Stringed

Medieval instruments can be constructed for decorative purposes. Strings can be fitted and plucked to mime an actual (hidden) instrument or recording.

Lute

study paintings, drawings or photographs for decoration and colours of all instruments

drill holes for strings

thick card strips for body – overlap, glue and pin to edge of sound board

pegs – large wooden beads or small discs – use long screws

glued string decoration

carved curved back

notches for strings

recess to thickness of soundboard

top view of finger board

mortice for peg board tenon

sound board and formers – plywood or board

20 strings on lutes but 10/12 is practical

A scene from 'Adventure Story' (see also page 140) showing one of the characters 'playing' the lyre.

drill holes for nylon or cord strings

glued felt or bead

thin felt edge

dowel

plywood or board

thin plywood or hardboard

wood blocks

holes for dowel

Lyre

Wind instruments and drums

cut card cone glued to wire ring and dowel

tape

Roman buccina

card cone taped to tube

either metal tube or plastic hose with wire inside to help retain the shape

glued felt

Long horns   Use existing coach horn if available.

25 mm. dowel

glued felt mouth-piece

glued felt or washers

bent metal tube into dowel

adhesive tape

wires forced into tube

plastic or rubber tube with heavy gauge wire inside before bending retains shape ~ metal tube alternative

wire frame soldered to wire rim or tie with tape

glued felt decorations

wire

Early horn or trumpet

38 mm. dowel

brass scrap for keys, etc.

plastic tub as basic shape to build bell of trumpet

18th century basset horn

Simple pipe

bamboo

cork into end and shape with saw

bell shape~ use suitable knob or turn on lathe

paint and decorate top layer of papier mâché

large cardboard cylinder base

layers of paper to build up curve

large stoneware jar (not suitable for playing)

plastic sheet or old rubber inner tube

threaded string

Drums

Use existing instruments if available.

large preserve tin or cardboard cylinder

large cardboard cylinder base

string or cord

cake tin

Side drum   **Two-ended drum**   **Indian drum**   **African drum**

THE BOX

Caskets and jewel boxes

folded card shaped for top of boxes

shaped for beading

exploded view of casket illustrated below left.

25 mm. softwood

25 mm. expanded polystyrene ~ P.V.A. adhesive to fix ~ an overlaid muslin glued into shapes will protect the surface.

4 mm. plywood base

decorate boxes with metallic paints ~ (old gold, silver, bronze, etc.) underpaint with dark brown, grey, brown respectively.

paper pulp with lacquer paint finish

glued string surround 'jewels'

card tops

painted decoration

wood blocks or metal scrap

sized felt

glued string or cord

All boxes can be decorated over existing boxes or constructed as shown above.

The chest

Large decorative boxes can be created out of existing old trunks or chests.

finish all felt decorations with a coat or two of clear shellac

Medieval chest

old metal trunk

bottle tops, buttons etc. on sized felt strip

sized felt decorations on painted lacquer or enamal background

Renaissance chest

felt strips

feet~wood blocks

painted decorations

old travelling trunk

A coffin

A simple, plain shape, as used in a production of 'Oliver'. More ornate designs should be built over a simple shape with wood mouldings, and gilded as required.

handles~heavy gauge wire: entwine with sized felt and paint with metallic colour

paper pulp knob

hinge or metal strip

25 mm. plywood or blockboard

roundel~hardboard or plywood base, screwed through trunk to wood blocks inside

drill holes for split pins ~washers inside

16 mm. blockboard or plywood

wood strips for mouldings paint on patterns

felt or scrap materials~use P.V.C. adhesive

ram's head in paper pulp, edging in thick cord, background painted pattern.

PAPER PROPS

Scrolls

1 Soften the edges or make ragged by tearing.

2 Colour with very thin uneven washes of ochres and pale greys.

3 Pull paper under a straight-edge when it is dry in order to effect curl.

polystyrene block

lino block

thin cut paper

roller for pressure

block

roller for inking

sheet of glass

LINO PAINT

Paper money

1 Printing block of expanded polystyrene carved by electric cutter.

2 Quantity of thin paper cut to size.

3 Rollers for printing and pressing down.

Books

If books are to be very large and dominant on stage, it will be preferable to seek out old dilapidated ones at jumble sales and secondhand shops. They can be repaired and decorated with felt, cord, beads, etc. and then painted and shellac varnished if required.

cut felt glued to cover

Letters and documents

They can be made in the same way as scrolls (without curling) and then ribboned together for bundles.

QUILLS AND INKWELLS

Select some goose quills and any small pot. It may be possible to obtain an old style of inkwell but an easy method of construction is shown below.

pheasant feather

goose feather

thick cord or felt rim

glued tissue helps retain rim

felt strip

plywood base

card surround to ink bottle

blockboard or plywood base

FOOD AND KITCHEN WARE

If a feast is to be held on stage, many of the items can be made in the workshop. Grapefruit, oranges, pumpkins, melons and other large fruits of a more or less spherical shape can be modelled over old plastic balls using papier mâché, or can be constructed in the wire and paper methods described on previous pages. Bananas, root vegetables and more elongated forms can be built from paper pulp, wire and papier mâché, or carved from expanded polystyrene. Grapes and smaller forms can be made with paper pulp built round fine wire.

Cheeses, cakes and other cylindrical forms can be made from round cake/biscuit tins, covered with plaster or paper and decorated.

Meats, poultry and all irregular forms can be constructed in foam rubber, expanded polystyrene or by the wire frame and papier mâché method. Plaster-of-Paris is useful for icing and creams.

Brush all surfaces with shellac for a bright, fresh appearance and to fix all colours.

Bread can be used after painting over with a coat of clear shellac.

Edible foods can be arranged among the 'prop' foods if eating is required. Care should be taken when choosing food from the table!

Cooking utensils, crockery, etc. can usually be obtained and used as found. A slight change of tone and colour may be necessary. If changes of style are necessary to suggest an earlier period, handles, spouts and other fittings can be attached to metal with P.V.A. adhesives. Such additions can be fashioned from wire and paper pulp as previously described and should be painted to match the basic article.

cut paper roll glued into 'fruit'

felt pieces

vegetables built up with paper pulp or polystyrene

shellfish ~ actual specimen cleaned out ~ or paper pulp

paper pulp built round fine wire for small fruits

spherical shaped fruits ~ papier mâché over old balls

pastry ~ shapes in cut felt

plaster icing

cake tin

butter muslin

actual loaves or paper pulp

cylindrical forms (cakes, cheeses, pastries) use cake tin foundation.

boar's head, meats & poultry ~ use papier mâché over fine wire mesh frame and wood structure

muslin

screwed newspaper

wood block

papier mâché over chicken wire and board structure

plywood or hardboard

172

Lighting 7

LAMPS AND EQUIPMENT · COLOUR · POSITIONING

STAGE LIGHTING EQUIPMENT

The light source

Before you can plan a layout for your lighting it is necessary to know the limits of your electrical supply. Once you know the amount of your supply in amp(ere)s (x amps per socket) it is simply a matter of using the formula 'watts divided by volts equals amps'. For example, if your voltage is 240 and you wish to use lamps with a total wattage of 9600, you will need at least 40 amps in reserve. If the lighting operator already knows these facts, dangers of overloading can be avoided.

Above: medium pre-focus cap (P28) Projection lamp

Above: G.L.S. lamp Edison screw

Lamp types

Three main groups are in use in the theatre: the General Lighting Service (G.L.S.) which is Tungsten, the Projection Lamp which is Tungsten, and the Tungsten Halogen Lamp. The G.L.S. is used in batten and flood lanterns, the Projection and Tungsten Halogen in spot lanterns. Illustrations on the right show the most commonly used lamps, their dimensions and type of base fitting.

Fittings are as follows:

1 Edison or Giant Edison screw (E.S. or G.E.S.) G.L.S. lamps in older floods and compartment battens.
2 Class K lamps (double ended) in newer floods.
3 Pre-focus caps (P28 or P40) on Projection lamps in spot lanterns.
4 Twin pins for Tungsten Halogen lamps in spot lanterns.
5 PAR 64 Sealed beam in Parcans.

Above: 500w or 1000w Class K Linfar filament lamp
Right: 1000w PAR 64 sealed beam lamp

The lantern

To give direction and control, the lamps are fitted within a variety of casings, called lanterns. The lamp is backed by a reflector which directs the light in a wide or narrow angled beam.

The lanterns fall into two main groups, known as *floods* and *spots*. The floods cast light over a wide area, whereas the spots use a lens to concentrate light on a selected small area of the stage.

Above: 1000w class T/9 Tungsten Halogen lamp
Below: New generation compact filament lamp

Telescopic stand, with single extension. Can be supplied with castors.

Floods

Floodlights are the large reflector units with a fixed wide angle beam that illuminate large areas of the stage or cyclorama.

They are most useful as a form of general lighting for the backing, whether a backcloth, cyclorama or backing flat behind the door or window of an interior set.

The units are suspended above the stage or attached to a mobile, telescopic stand. They can be swivelled and tilted but there is no adjustment for the size of the beam and consequently no possibility to make the lit area larger or smaller.

For many years the light source in a flood was a G.L.S. lamp backed by a simple reflector. Such floods are no longer manufactured but many remain in use.

The batten

The other type of general lighting is supplied by the batten. This consists of several small floods joined together. They are usually suspended on bars above and at the base of the backcloth or cyclorama, at a distance of 1 m – in the latter position on stage they are termed 'ground-row', not to be confused with scenic ground-rows (see glossary page 270). Each batten is wired in three or four circuits so that different colour filters can be used with each circuit.

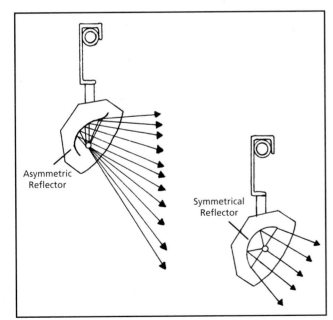

Modern floods use linear filament lamps and a choice of reflectors offering either a symmetric or asymmetric beam. The vertical spread of asymmetric beams is particularly useful for lighting cycloramas at close range.

Traditional batten – 3 circuit/3 colour with 100/150 watt lamps.

Coda 4 – a modern batten (4 circuit/4 colour) with asymmetric reflectors.

batten lamp holders

50×50 mm. cable trunking

lids cut with tin-snips ~ filters taped inside edges

3 circuits

Left: A home-made compartment batten, using biscuit/cake tins as reflectors and the lids with pieces cut out to accommodate colour filters. This batten, and another similar, lit the cyclorama for 'Fiddler on the Roof' – see pages 26 and 70.

Above: 650w Quartet PC

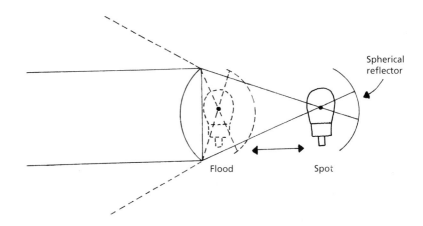

Spherical reflector

Flood

Spot

Above: Simple focus spots have either a fixed plano convex (P.C.) or stepped (fresnel) lens. When lamp and reflector are moved towards or away from the lens, the beam becomes wider or narrower.

Right: 1200w Cantata PC (left) and Fresnel (right) spot. A four-leaf barndoor can be fitted to PC and Fresnel spots to shape the beam.

All spotlights on pages 176 and 177 are from Strand Lighting

Spots – Focus (P.C. Fresnel and Profile)

The spotlights are the second group of lanterns – a type that can be focused, unlike the floods which belong to the 'fixed' group. The advantage of spreading the light to meet particular requirements is gained by altering the relationship between the lamp and a lens.

Spots themselves fall into two groups:

Fresnel or 'soft edge' which throw a soft-edged beam, and Profile which produce a beam which can be focused to provide a hard or soft edge to the beam. The simple spots (shown on the opposite page) vary the beam by moving the lamp and reflector in relation to the lens – see diagram left. The Profile spots below use the lens to focus a variable shaped gate through which light is directed by a reflector system – see diagram right.

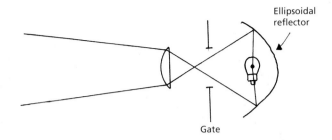

Above: The lamp and reflector of a profile spot are fixed; the lens is moved to harden or soften the beam which is sized and shaped by four shutter blades in the gate position.

Below: Some profiles have two independently moveable lenses in a zoom arrangement to provide a wider range of beam angles.

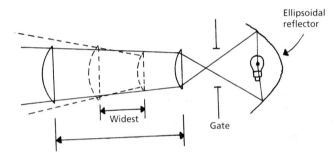

Far left: Quartet profile spot (650w). Available with beam angle zooming from 15° to 25° or from 22° to 40°.

Left: SL profile spot with a highly efficient optical system and a new generation 600w lamp which provides a light output exceeding that of a standard 1000w profile. Available in a series of fixed beam angles.

Left: Cantata profile spots (1200w) zooming from 18° to 32° or from 26° to 44°.

Right: SL zoom profile spot. Available with beam angle zooming from 15° to 32° or from 23° to 50°.

177

Parcans

The Parcan is perhaps the brightest, simplest, and cheapest lighting instrument available. Like the flood it cannot be focused. But, unlike the flood, it has a very narrow beam and so provides a very directional light. It is called a Parcan because all the optics, including the near-parabolic reflector are sealed in the PAR 64 lamp which looks rather like a car headlight. So only a simple can-like housing is required to provide pan (left/right) and tilt (up/down) movements. The Parcan is the favourite light for pop and rock concerts but it is also very useful for all kinds of performance – particularly for side and back light. The 1000w lamps are available as narrow beam (CP61), medium beam (CP62) and wide beam (CP63). The beams are slightly oval and the lamp can be rotated within the can to make the best use of this oval shape. The intense brightness allows the use of strongly saturated colour filters without the loss of light associated with dense filters in conventional spotlights. But – remember! – Parcans offer no control of the beam size or beam shape other than by choice of lamp!

A Parcan

408 Ocelot (small)   974 Hong Kong

410 Ocelot (large)   304 Arc de Triomphe

Gobos

Gobos

Profile spotlights may be used to project line images which have been cut in thin heat-resistant metal. These are called gobos (nobody knows where the word comes from!) and must be placed in the 'gate' which is a slot next to the shutters. Gobos may be used to project clean images such as city skylines and windows or, softly focused, to give broken texture to the light. A favourite use is to dapple the light as if it were passing through trees. Manufacturers have extensive catalogues of standard gobos but simple break-ups (and even windows – if you have a steady hand!) can be cut from aluminium oven pie dishes. When using soft focus, interesting effects can be obtained using a split filter – i.e. two different coloured gels butt-joined together, vertically, horizontally or diagonally.

Focusing

- When focusing a light for an acting area, stand with your back to the light so that you are not blinded. If you can see a full shadow plus a little bit of light above the shadow of your head, you will be lit. If some of the actors are taller than you, allow for a bit more height.
- Move around in the beam to check that an actor will be lit everywhere in the area that the spotlight is intended to cover.
- Give clear instructions to the person handling the spotlight. Talk in terms of the adjustments that are possible – up/down, left/right and big/small. Then adjust barndoors or shutters, if available. Finally, if it is a profile spot, adjust the hard/soft.
- Profile spots are normally focused softly to make the edge as unobtrusive as possible. Audience eyes are pulled towards a hard edge and, perhaps consciously but mostly sub-consciously, the brain tries to work out a reason. To avoid distraction, always have a reason (sun or moon through a window or door?) for a hard edge.
- Diffusion filters can be useful for softening light and the diffusers known as *silks* also stretch the light in any direction chosen according to the way the filter is cut and framed. This can be very useful when equipment is in short supply. The material is the plastic of normal filters but is called silk because it has fine lines running through it.

Safety

Safety is largely a matter of common sense. Most accidents arising from lighting are mechanical rather than electrical – usually caused by lack of care while under pressure to get the lights ready in time for rehearsal. Electrical matters are subject to specific regulations but this does not remove the need for vigilance in common-sense matters.

- Check all hanging clamps are tightened.
- Ensure 'Safeties' (chains or wires) are always fitted.
- Always observe manufacturers' recommendations for access equipment (towers, steps or ladders).
- Never go up a ladder unless someone is 'footing' the bottom.
- Never ever leave tools at the top of ladders.
- Never interfere with permanent wiring of the stage.
- Ensure regular maintenance. In the UK all spotlights are subject to Portable Appliance Testing regulations.
- Scheduled maintenance and testing does not remove the need for continual vigilance, particularly visual checks to ensure (A) no physical damage to spotlights or cables and (B) outer sheaths of cables are securely clamped where they enter plugs so that no strain is placed on the individual wire connections.
- Before changing a lamp, always unplug the spotlight and allow time for the glass to cool.

Pack with six 2500w dimmers and twinned socket outlets allowing two lights to be fed from each dimmer. A single dimmer pack (below left) may be controlled by a simple box with six faders and a master fader such as the Act 6 (below right), or several packs may be controlled from a desk such as the LX (below far right).

Lighting control equipment

All systems now use electronic dimmers operated from remote-control desks. Standard dimmers will control up to 2500w, so it is possible to use more than one light on a dimmer provided that care is taken not to exceed the individual load for each dimmer and the maximum available power supply. Most simple manual systems allow one lighting picture to be prepared in advance but the digital memory of more advanced systems allows a virtually unlimited number of light changes to be programmed at the lighting rehearsal and stored for replay at performance.

Computer based control desks such as the Strand GSX (below) allow lighting pictures to be memorised in rehearsal for playback in performance.

Two preset desks such as the Strand LX (below) allow two light pictures to be prepared in advance and then brought to the stage by operating the master faders.

POSITIONING

for proscenium and apron stages

The tubular 'barrels' suspended between the borders (when in position, called 'bars') provide support for all lamps above the stage. On very small stages only a No. 1 bar position is needed, whereas large stages will need two or three positions.

The most used position is always No. 1 bar immediately behind the proscenium arch, as this carries the lamps for the centre stage area as well as for downstage left and right. The lanterns normally clamped here will be a variety of soft and hard edge spots. The hook clamp normally used for hanging lights is designed to fit a bar of standard scaffolding diameter.

Booms are barrels fixed in a vertical position. The spots can swivel on brackets clamped to these vertical bars. Booms are necessary on the larger stage – a small stage can use telescopic stage stands.

Sometimes a 'ladder' is suspended from No. 2 or No. 3 bar to carry lamps between the wings when additional light is required on centre stage.

Wall brackets are used to carry front-of-house (F.O.H.) lighting for illuminating downstage and the apron.

Consideration must now be given to the placing of spots, floods and battens about the stage and in the auditorium.

The illustration above shows the main areas of a proscenium stage that require lighting (the proscenium arch is not marked).

The areas are conveniently grouped as follows:

a the centre stage

b downstage and apron

c upstage

d the cyclorama

e backings

Most lighting is directed diagonally across the stage to avoid 'flattening' the setting and actors.

Side view of the stage and part of the auditorium stripped of all scenery, curtains, borders and wings in order to show the supporting apparatus for stage lighting.

3 or 4 circuit battens for N°.2 bar (No3. on larger stage)

500 W Fresnel spots for No 1 bar (and N°.2 bar) or perch

1000 W profile spot (or two 500w) for centre F.O.H.

No2. bar on larger stage

curtain back cloth or cyclorama

500/650 w Fresnel (tungsten halogen) with barn doors)

500 W profile spots – F.O.H. (also on No.1 bar if required)

F.O.H. SIDE WALL POSITION

BACK WALL (or BALCONY) POSITION

scenic groundrow

patch panel

dips

1000 W or 500 W floods on telescopic stage stands behind flats/wings for backings, etc.

'cylo' trough used as a ground row

stage dip boxes for protected plug points on permanent stages and patch panels for temporary arrangements

CENTRE – a mixture of Fresnel and P.C. and profile lamps on No. 1 bar.
DOWNSTAGE and APRON – front-of-house lighting using profile spots, one centred in hall for a larger apron.

UPSTAGE – on small stages: No. 1 bar with Fresnel or P.C. angled to upstage.
– on larger stages: No. 2 bar with two Fresnel or P.C. and two profile lamps.

CYCLORAMA and BACKINGS – two or more compartment battens and/or small floods.

Above: elevation   *Below: plan*

Number of lamps and number of circuits

On the smaller stage, as shown here, eleven spots, two floods and two 3-circuit battens are positioned. An alternative to the battens on No. 2 bar would be four or five spots and floods equal to the same wattage. If you have available a large number of Fresnels and no floods or battens, try to utilise these lights and make your own arrangement.

The number of circuits is dependent on the type of dimmer control used and the number and wattage of the lamps. A 6-way provides six dimmers, each dimmer feeding two sockets giving a total of twelve circuits. This system is capable of supplying up to twenty-four 500w or 650w lamps and will serve the spots, floods and battens shown in this small stage arrangement, allowing approximately 3kw in reserve for additional lamps.

Lamp symbols used in the plans and elevation:

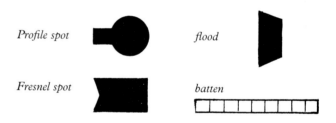

Profile spot   *flood*

Fresnel spot   *batten*

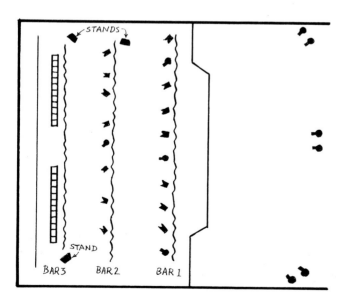

A larger stage will probably require about twenty-seven lamps (excluding battens) to give the same balance of intensity as on the smaller stage above. Note that there are six F.O.H. spots, No. 1 bar carries ten spots, No. 2 bar eight spots, No. 3 bar two battens and the stage stands three floods.

If 500w or 650w lamps are used for this arrangement, then a 12-way system will be needed. This will allow approximately 8kw in reserve for any additional lamps.

POSITIONING
for arena stages

In arena productions, it is important to avoid light beams that cause discomfort to the audience. Lanterns have to be focused with great care to cover the stage without any spillage beyond. Barn doors are invaluable for this purpose.

Another problem arises over suspension. If the production is to be staged in a hall regularly used for such events, wall brackets can be fitted; if in a temporary place (possibly at a local youth club for one night only), then some means of portable telescopic stands will be more suitable.

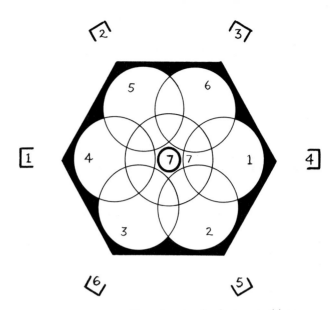

Plan view showing lantern positions.

It is preferable to direct the beam of each lantern diagonally across, as shown on the plan above and in the general view on the left. This avoids the heavy shadows on actors' faces from a light source directly above them. Spots are the most practical lanterns for the purpose as their beams can be focused accurately. Floods should be avoided.

183

COLOUR THEORY AND PRACTICE

This book deliberately concentrates on the practical aspects of stage craft. However, where colour is concerned (whether of light or of pigment) it is necessary to give a few notes on colour theory.

Light (daylight or sunlight) is white or 'colourless' until the light waves are separated. When any white light is split up by a prism the constituent colours emerge.

To get the colour required from a lamp a filter is fitted that allows only the colour of the filter to penetrate: a blue filter will absorb green, yellow, orange and red waves and allow the blue waves to 'reflect' on to the stage.

Colour filters work in much the same way as colour pigments. A blue pigment, for example, will absorb yellow, orange, red and green, and reflect the blue waves back to our retinas.

These two diagrams may help:

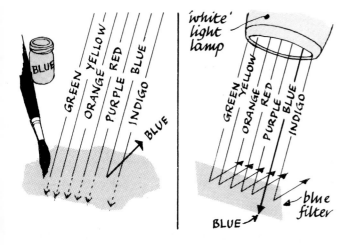

So an object seen as BLUE absorbs all other colours and a light seen as BLUE has had all other colours removed. An object or light reflecting all colour waves is seen as WHITE.

The two diagrams below show the difference in colour mixing between pigment and light.

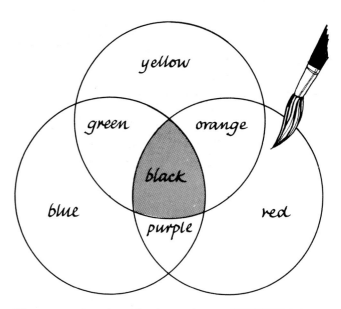

Pigment: primaries mixed together = GREY/BLACK

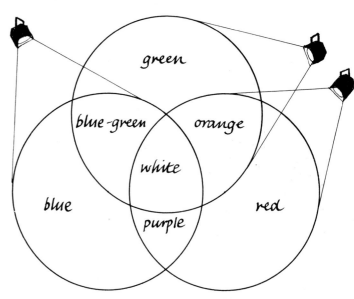

Light: primaries mixed together = WHITE

Note that light and pigment primaries differ in one respect – yellow is replaced by green in light.

Coloured light on coloured surfaces

The effect of a coloured light on coloured settings and costumes can be best explained by a further diagram:

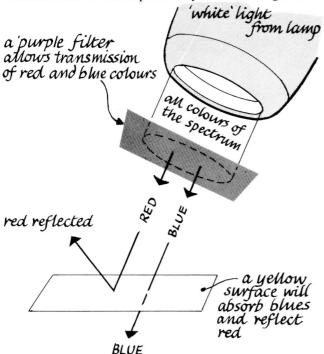

'white' light from lamp

a 'purple filter allows transmission of red and blue colours

all colours of the spectrum

red reflected

RED

BLUE

a yellow surface will absorb blues and reflect red

BLUE

In the illustration above, a purple light is seen as red on reflection. A yellow pigment reflects yellow, orange and red and absorbs blue – a purple light falling on such a surface will appear as RED, since the blue will be absorbed and the red reflected.

The general principles can be applied to any colour of light falling on any other colour of pigment. Here is a chart showing only primary colours of light falling on primary colours of pigment:

PIGMENT	LIGHT		
	red	green	blue
red	red	dark brown	dark purple
yellow	red	green	black
blue	black	green/blue	blue

Note: these colours are approximate only, depending entirely on the purity of light and pigment.

Colour mixing

The practical application of the colour mixing of primaries is best seen with cyclorama batten lighting where red, green and blue compartments are mixed in varying proportions by dimmers to produce any hue or tint in the spectrum.

If lights are hired from suppliers, the colours usually fitted to battens are primary red, green and blue. These will produce a satisfactory white light from a 3-circuit batten but it will be noted that the blue will be of lesser intensity. This is because of the weakness of blue light waves in tungsten filament lamps. (These lamps are in general use for battens. The tungsten halogen lamp eliminates the blue light wave problem.) To compensate for this loss, it is advisable to increase the wattage of lamps in the 'blue' circuit. The colours just mentioned are suitable for use on the cyclorama for sky or for symbolic background effects. But these filters, because of their depth of colour, are not really adequate for lighting the general acting area which demands a greater intensity of light. Other filters will be found preferable.

To avoid waste of light, use either of the following groups in battens for lighting acting areas:

1 No. 136 pale lavender, 103 straw, 117 steel blue
2 No. 192 flesh pink, 151 gold, 132 medium blue

All the primary light waves are included in these two groups and much better illumination will result.

Apart from cyclorama lighting, primary colours are also effective for revues, pantomime, musical plays and symbolic lighting.

Note: Colour numbers above and on the following page are from the Lee range. Other manufacturers (e.g. Rosco) have similar colours but different numbers.

Colour selection

Colour filters, which are sheets of gelatine or acetate, are sold under the trade name Cinemoid in two sizes. (The large sheet will make 12 batten filters, the small sheet 6 filters.) Over sixty colours are available from the suppliers (see page 276) and the problem is to select a limited number to meet the requirements of a particular production.

Successful choice will come with experience but a guide to essential filters will be helpful to those who have not experimented with lighting. Very few tints and primaries are needed, provided that a balance is achieved between warm and cool tints. The most useful for a small production or curtain set are:

No.			
103	straw (warm)	152	pale gold
117	steel blue (cool)	153	pale salmon
258	frost	154	pale rose
007	pale yellow		

258 light frost is useful for softening the edges of spotlights, either with or without the colour filter. (Frost does not affect the colour of the light.)

Below is a useful selection of filters for a more ambitious production:

103	straw	139	primary green
108	orange	140	pale blue
106	primary red	007	pale yellow
192	flesh pink	151	gold tint
110	middle rose	152	pale gold
115	peacock blue	153	pale salmon
116	blue green	154	pale rose
117	steel blue	156	chocolate
119	dark blue (as alternative to primary)	079	sky blue
136	pale lavender		

Amber is better avoided as it tends to spoil all cool colours in costumes and settings.

Sources of visible light

General lighting creates mood and atmosphere but the source of light for night scenes (interior and exterior) must be particularly well planned.

The fireplace, standard and wall lights, and chandelier lighting – for modern plays – and fireplace, torch, gas mantle and oil lamps – for earlier periods – can give great emphasis to a scene.

For standard and wall-bracket lighting, suitable spots with warm colour filters must be directed to the areas of supposed light, the actual light or lights in the setting only having a low-wattage or 'pygmy' lamp. The small lamps can be fitted into a gas mantle, as an oil 'wick' or under a lampshade on a wall light. Candles are best fitted with battery and bulb as illustrated on page 139, unless special fire precautions are taken for using real candles.

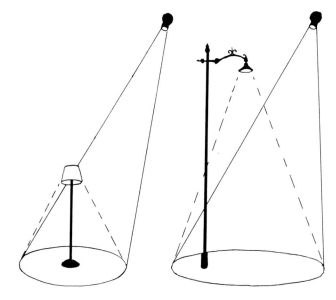

Supposed light areas from spotlights.

Special optical effects are beyond the scope of this book. If methods of projecting light on to cyclorama, showing slides, etc. are required contact one of the stage lighting suppliers listed on page 276.

DESIGNING THE LIGHTING LAYOUT

The approaches to lighting a play will be as many and as varied as there are designers and directors. Some directors will depend entirely on the visual concept from the designer whilst others may submit rough sketches or a plan of their own for the designer to develop.

A Shakespearean play with its many scenes will obviously require more thought to be given to variety of lighting than, say, a revue sketch. But even a short revue or one-act play will demand equal care in the placing of the lights.

Priorities in placing the lights

The priorities are:

1 to light the actors, especially their faces. The actors must *show* what they are thinking, feeling and saying;

2 to enhance the grouping of actors on the stage, so that certain of the characters dominate by virtue of suitable lighting as well as costume;

3 to illuminate the set;

4 to indicate time and season;

5 to set a mood or atmosphere.

Plan the lighting carefully to suit the movement of actors around the stage, avoiding 'black spots' where an actor cannot be properly seen.

There must be sufficient light to make the settings convincing in atmosphere and contrast. Remember that contrast is of prime importance, that variety of light in different areas of the stage is most essential for dramatic impact.

Lighting the cyclorama

An important role in dramatic lighting is played by the placing of cyclorama lights.

If used without front lighting, a silhouette is achieved.

The scene on the right (from a production of 'The Tempest') illustrates the use of the cyclorama at the beginning of a scene or play – the cyclorama is lit by a top batten and two side floods.

Back lighting

Other dramatic effects are achieved by combining cyclorama lights with spots directed *forward* towards the downstage. In a scene requiring strong sunlight a 1000w flood, together with a Fresnel, was directed downstage on to the temple wall to the right of the head of Apollo. Battens lit the cyclorama (in this case, the wall of the hall). Always ensure that such lighting does not spill into the audience.

Left and bottom left: the scene shows the temple at Delphi from 'Adventure Story'. As Alexander climbs over a sculptured sill by the statue of Apollo, the sun strikes his back, casting his shadow on the temple wall. The priestess downstage is softly illuminated by profile and Fresnel spots.

Below right: a scene from 'West Side Story' shows the use of back and front lighting with a dark centre stage area – a use of localised lighting for a dramatic purpose.

Lighting plan for Act I Scene 2 of 'Adventure Story'.

188

Positioning lights in a limited stage space

On very small stages and where no space is available for 'flies' (galleries above the stage area of the same height as the stage area itself) or for hanging lights from above, lanterns must be carefully placed behind flats and in the auditorium.

In the illustrations on this page, note the nearness of ceiling to stage level. In the scene from 'Julius Caesar' the lanterns are grouped immediately behind the narrow temporary proscenium arch (which does not appear in the picture) and in F.O.H. positions. The main light source is on stage left – note the shadows.

Scene before battle in Shakespeare's 'Julius Caesar' (a school production with arms and armour made in the school workshop. See pages 202–203.)

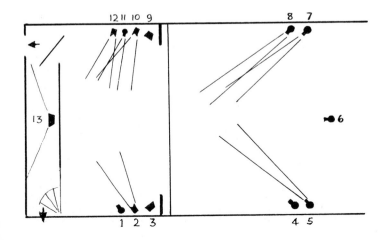

Left: diagrammatic plan of lighting for the scene above, with switched-on lighting indicated by beam lines in the diagram. Most lights, because of the lack of space, are situated behind the proscenium arch (built up from flats – see page 14). The battens are fixed vertically (3 and 9) on booms. The scene is lit mainly from stage left with 7 and 8 F.O.H., 10, 11, and 12; 2 is lit on stage right and 5 F.O.H.; 13 is a large 1000w flood placed behind the large wall-flat to illuminate the back wall. If the colour of an existing wall is pale in tint, it is often possible, as in this case, to light direct without a curtain or backcloth.

Light positioning for 'Oliver' in a small hall

Below is a plan view of light positions for a particular production. All available lights were placed in the most advantageous positions to ensure that all essential acting areas were covered. A variety of gels (colour filters) were fitted to enable the changing moods to be created effectively.

Plan for the workhouse setting in Act I Scene I of 'Oliver' by Lionel Bart.

Act I Scene 1: workhouse.

Act I Scene 2: workhouse parlour.

Act I Scenes 3 and 4: street and undertaker's.

Act I Scene 5: Paddington Green.

Act I Scene 6: Thieves' kitchen.

Act II Scene I: Inn.

Act II Scene 2: Brownlow's house.

Final scene: riverside.

The eight small sketches above illustrate the variations obtainable with the lights arranged as in the diagram on the left (variations in colour are not shown, of course). The sketches show eight scenes from 'Oliver'. (See also pages 74–75 on sketch methods.) On the next page the placing of the lights is explained in relation to certain requirements and priorities.

This illustration explains the lighting for the scene below. F.O.H. lights **4** and **5** illuminate the group of workhouse boys, whilst Oliver is emphasised by an additional Fresnel spot **(2)** from above stage right. A profile 500w spot **(1)** lights part of the background wall.

Left: a scene from the musical 'Oliver'. Note how Oliver, the main character, is made the focal point of the lighting in this scene.

THE LIGHTING REHEARSAL

Before the lighting rehearsal the director should give the chief electrician some idea of the quantity of light that he would like for each scene, the moods he wants to create, the time of day, the place and any particular effects (e.g. a fire, a thunderstorm). The electricians will also need to know the placing of windows, doors, furniture and the main acting areas.

When the relevant facts are established, the electricians can check the equipment available and hire additional lamps, dimmers and 'gels'.

All lights will be placed before the rehearsal, focused on the most useful area. Appropriate gels can be fitted. Each light should be given a number and the number marked on a sketch plan for reference and easy plotting during the rehearsal.

The lighting rehearsal (continued)

When such arrangements have all been made, the producer and designer should each be informed of the number and colour positions of each light on a sketch plan.

Finally before the rehearsal, make sure that the electricians have a comprehensive list of all the effects needed, including sound effects; also a text with sound cues, exits and entrances marked – indeed anything that may affect the work of the electricians.

The director and designer should be present at the rehearsal, together with some members of the cast dressed in costume. The latter can move, sit or stand in appropriate positions to ensure that the lights cover them and create around them the desired mood.

It is essential to mark clearly in the margins of the text script every light, sound and other effect. If there is to be a slow dimming of the light over two and a half pages, indicate in the margin with a long arrow from the start of the appropriate cue.

Two important points: unless a sudden change of light is relevant, always fade lights in and out slowly – if lights 'jump in' the effect is spoilt and the audience is distracted; when a blackout is required, ensure that it is a blackout – no working lights left on!

Working at the lighting plot

Start with a blackout and gradually bring up the lights to the required setting for the play to open – this is usually called the pre-setting and is visible to the audience on arrival. Mark this on the script as Cue 1, noting on the plot the exact number of lights and their exact dimmer calibrations. You then move on to the next cue – and so on throughout the play. Always note exactly which lights are added and which removed, also which lights are changed to a higher or lower dimmer calibration.

During the lighting rehearsal give yourself time to experiment in order to achieve the best effect. If the number of lights is small, be prepared to change positions and gels.

A typical lighting plot will look rather like this:

Cue No.	CUE	Preset 'A'								Preset 'B'					
		Master	1	2	3	4	5	6	Master	1	2	3	4	5	6
1	presetting	full	0	0	0	0	4	0	off	0	0	0	0	0	0
*2	houselights fade as music builds up	full	0	0	0	0	3	0	off	0	0	0	0	0	0
*3	curtain up slow fade in	full	3	7	F	F	F	7	full	3	0	0	7	4	0
4	Mr Brown enters	full	3	F	F	F	F	F	full	3	0	0	7	4	0
5	Elizabeth exits, begin sunset	full	3	F	F	6	F	7	full	0	0	0	4	4	0
5a	sunset complete (3 pages text)	full	3	F	F	6	F	7	off	0	0	0	0	0	0
6	blackout	off	0	F	F	6	F	7	off	0	0	0	0	0	0

*if there is no curtain, cues **2** and **3** crossfade, i.e. **2** goes down as **3** comes up. F = full on.

Arms and armour

8

ARMATURES AND DUMMIES · ARMOUR THROUGH THE AGES · WEAPONS AND GUNS

COSTUME ARMOUR

A comprehensive range of excellent illustrated books is available to anyone seeking methods of making stage costumes – the variety is such that no additional material is necessary in this book – see the book list on page 277.

However, there is a definite lack of information about techniques for making armour, whether the basic leather jacket or the elaborate plate armour of the sixteenth century. Most costume books make some textual reference but there is little in the way of illustrations from which to work.

This section on arms and armour is, therefore, an attempt to rectify the situation, showing the development of arms and armour by grouping them into historical periods, and showing methods of construction and decoration. Most of the examples can be made by school-children but care must be exercised in measurements and in securing the fixing points. Where a very high standard of finish is desirable, or time and labour demands a quick solution, costume armour can be hired – see the list of suppliers on page 276.

On the next few pages a group of dummies is shown. They serve as supports for building up the various pieces of armour subsequently shown.

DUMMIES FOR BREAST ARMOUR

Ideally an old adjustable shop dummy or tailor's dummy is most suitable but a strong well-shaped dummy can be built as shown. It may be necessary to make three sizes: large, medium and small if a large cast of military is demanded. Measure the actors involved.

When the final covering of scrim in plaster has been applied, the dimensions can be made more accurate, or adjusted, by applying papier mâché pulp and paper.

The whole surface should be painted with enamel paint when it has dried out. Waxing or varnishing afterwards will produce a surface ideal for repeated use and resistant to glues.

plywood disc for neck position supported on angled piece of 50×50 mm softwood

2 plywood discs for arm positions

3 vertical frame members – 50×25 mm

heavy gauge wire

3 horizontal frame members ~50×50 mm

secure frame with tape

25 mm blockboard or plywood base plate

staples

large pieces of sugar paper for finish
paper mâché layers over scrim
hessian scrim dipped in plaster

medium wire mesh stapled and tied to wood and wire framework

Basic breast garment over the dummy

The basic garment for all breast armour: an old blanket (or similar material) is cut as below, in one piece to the required length for back and front. The neck opening can be cut square or circular as required. Shoulder pieces may be used to widen and/or strengthen the armour.

surface sanded down and painted with lacquer or enamel

three coats of shellac

neck opening

2 shoulder pieces

Leg and arm dummies

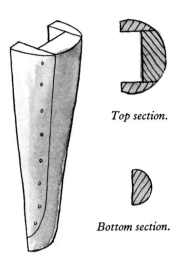

Top section.

Bottom section.

Three pieces – two of 75 × 25 mm, one of 50 × 75 mm – glue together.

Tie together and plane to shape.

Final dummy – nail and glue parts together.

The basic greave or lower leg armour

layer of greaseproof paper

card strips prevent crushing

To make leg armour, cover dummies with a sheet of greaseproof paper, to prevent armour from sticking to dummies.

For the armour, use corrugated cardboard, the first layer with the corrugations uppermost – glue the surface.

The second layer with corrugations down – glue the surface. Work the two layers into each other.

Finally tie dummy and cardboard together lightly. Leave for two or three days to dry thoroughly.

A dummy head (helmets)

The head armature is built on a 50 × 50 mm post, with any suitable base of approximately 30 cm square in plywood, blockboard or softwood. Four supporting braces of approximately 50 × 25 mm wood will prevent movement. The piping can be of lead, copper or other available metal or plastics, which should be wired and stapled as shown to the upper part of the post.

When the armature is complete, use galvanised wire, thin or medium gauge, and wire mesh over the whole surface. Snip and trim all protruding parts and cover with hessian scrim dipped in plaster of Paris. Use one layer without over-laying the pieces of scrim. Allow to dry and make quick check of measurements required. Apply further layers as necessary.

(See page 276 for scrim suppliers.)

When complete the head surface should be smoothed out with plaster and/or cotton scrim. *At all stages the measurements should not exceed those of the actor.*

So make sure that the armature is much smaller at the beginning. At the final stage the dummy head can be 1 cm larger in circumference to allow for shrinkage of helmet materials.

Steam felts over a can of boiling water, then press down firmly over a dummy. Repeat the process until the right shape is achieved.

Add nasals and cheek pieces with a hand-stapler. Pieces can be added or removed as required. Glue before stapling.

support felt hat for steaming on wire hook frame across top of can

Muslin applied with thin glue can be added on top of the felt and developed into the required period shape. Finish with paper and shellac.

Before using the dummy head, ensure that all measurements have been taken from the actor concerned. Helmet materials should be cut or fitted to the actor – this will not be possible with an old felt hat which has first to be steamed out (see above).

A large production, involving ten or more armour costumes, will require more than one dummy. If two or three are built, ensure that you make three sizes – large, medium and small – using the smaller with paper or felt padding to build up the in-between sizes of head measurement.

Also available from some hairdressers, haberdashers and local stores are cheap expanded polystyrene wig stands. They are adequate for small head sizes. Some means of securing to a base will be essential.

ANCIENT CIVILISATIONS

The chief form of defence for Old Testament and other early soldiers was the shield – then dagger, sword and javelin or spear. Body protection was of skins initially. Metal plates and tabs were added to the leather tunics later.

approx. 2 metre length spear - use 25mm dowel

large shield~bend hardboard as shown on page 213

rectangular quiver~ see page 215

build up with pulp & papier mâché over cap

crest of cut felt on wire frame & papier mâché

Babylonian daggers

taped wire and cord

plywood blades

Sumerian axe

felt bands over dowel - gold finish

metal disc

scale plates - paint in metal colours on long tunic

Sumerian soldier

Egyptian sword and shield

plywood

carved wood handle

cut egg box segments for studding

use flocking to simulate skin surface on hardboard shield

drill holes in wood disc to take arrows

corrugated card round 2 wooden discs ~ glue & tack

goose or hen feathers cut and glued to thin dowel

cut felt shoe and tape over front

Persian quiver and arrows

Assyrian archer

198

GAULS, SAXONS AND VIKINGS

Defensive equipment was basically similar to that of earlier peoples – the shield, often with a large boss was the main item. The helmet was probably worn only by leaders in battle. Metal strips and tabs were added to tunics to give added protection.

Viking helmets

felt bands over felt cap

cut felt glued to felt cap, shellac and paint in metallic finish

helmet construction basically as Roman (page 202)

wire frame and paper pulp horns ~ bend wires inside cap and glue felt patch to secure ends

Saxon armour

thick dowel shaft ~ tapered axe head ~ carve from block

either wire and papier mâché, hardboard or refuse bin lid

polystyrene/plastic etc., for bosses, string/cord patterns

wires

dowel

bottle tops or metal washers

stiffened felt or carved wood spearhead

card crest with tabs for glueing

plywood spearhead

25mm dowel shaft

sew wire frame to felt cap ~ papier mâché, sandpaper and shellac

long tunic (simulated leather)

sword and scabbard making see page 216

metallic discs - use paper pulp (page 234) or scrap metal oddments

metal arm bands (see Greek armour page 200)

metallic linked tabs (see page 236)

leather apron

brown tapes

soft shoes (moccasin type)

Gallic soldier

199

GREEKS - Armour

See page 212 for weapons.

expanded polystyrene cut out and set into wire frame support

papier mâché over wire mesh and wire frame

horse hair plumed crest →

felt cap method (see page 197)

arm bands of stiffened felt (shellac) tie elastic across gap

bronze painted finish to cuirass

under tunic

Helmet

tabs

cord and string

felt or pulp stud →

great crest of thick card - plume of hair etc., or painted

crest support: glue to helmet

felt edging glued and stapled

felt or cord across back

FOOT SOLDIERS

buckram heel support - sew to under sole

tapes or laces

greaves

OFFICER

200

thick felt or underfelt encased with muslin and shellac

pulp-metallic studs (page 236)

Breast armour

Ideally the breast plate or cuirass should be made with a thick felt base. However, various materials may be substituted which are cheaper to use – thick carpet underfelt (if backed with butter muslin) will survive a production, or two old blankets sewn together and stiffened with shellac. Try also foam rubber and other plastic materials.

cord edging

wire ties and cords to secure shoulder piece

Scale armour

two layers of old blanket sewn together and shellac

method N.º 1 – plates cut and sewn individually

method N.º 2 – plates cut in bands of felt

Breastplate (cuirass)

metal tabs (see page 236) glue to garment

how to overlap

tabs cut out – use sharp knife for thick material

shoulder pieces of thick felt – sewn to garment with 'rivets' of glue drops or paper fasteners

wide bands of felt or card sewn or stapled to undergarment

Greaves

cut from basic shape (see page 195 for construction)

glue and staple

pulp studding as above

cord edging

straps sewn or stapled after glueing

cord or rope for edging

CUT

201

ROMANS – Armour

Breast armour

Three types of breast armour are shown: plate, scale and cast plate (the last in two pieces worn by the officer).

Plate armour

A

with or without tabs

→ press studs

thick card

B

simple version of 'A' above – plates painted in metallic colours on stiff card – muslin edges to prevent tearing.

tabs glued and stapled

Scale armour

C

felt undergarment

scale plates in cut out bands or separate pieces of felt

Standards, spears and other arms on page 213.

see 'C' type armour below

closed position

STANDARD BEARER

felt cap built over dummy (see page 197)

felt pieces

wire frame, wire mesh and papier mâché

All armour: finish either in bronze, leather or bronzed-leather

(use metal powders described on page 111)

back fittings as front

socks under lacing

Soldier's helmet

boot laces or tapes

SOLDIER

202

plume of horsehair, trimmed bunch of feathers or other material

free interpretation of Officer's armour – large felt/card discs glued onto simulated leather jacket

Crested helmet

tape plume material to suitable shape

thick card cut to fit cap

decorations in cut felt and/or string

thick card or felt

thick string edging

glued string

Cloak

(paludamentum) worn over armour – fix with large brooch and wire

leather strap

greaves only occasionally worn – glue and sew/staple to inside

1 sword through gap

wood holder

2

Sword belts

Greaves

Officer's baton – use thick dowel and stud with nails

wire brooch to jacket

The breastplate
(cuirass or lorica).

tailored shape made from felt or doubled blanket stiffened with shellac – build over dummy (see page 195)

stiffened felt decorations

Brachiae
– a kind of breeches used for campaigns in the North – use cut jeans

Caligula in brown tapes or leather laces

straps and buckles sewn to outer side

felt, bottle tops or paper pulp ornaments

lower tabs – cut from one piece of felt; upper from separate pieces – glue & sew

OFFICER

203

ROMANESQUE AND EARLY GOTHIC ARMOUR

10 – 13th centuries: Normans

Swords and other weapons on pages 214 and 215.

Basic garment of hood and tunic was made of chain mail. Various helmets and scaled tunics were worn by knights over this mail.

stiffened felt nasal

A

pointed cone helmet - build up point in paper pulp on cap

laces

B

Helmets

A - conical type helmet and nasal
B - kettle hat type with card rim - cords glued over cap

Knitted mail should have links as large as possible, made with grey wool and sprayed with metallic silver. Alternatively, macramé (or knotting) may be used – see opposite page. Reference books on the technique should be available from libraries.

ARCHER

FOOT SOLDIER

mail armour

felt caps (page 197)

mail muffler drawn back over wrist

pulped paper built on felt cap

card

felt or card

thick knitting wool

thick socks over long hose

Kite shield

204

flat topped helmet

mail as shown opposite →

mail hood drawn back

Scale armour

An old jersey or jumper can be used as an undergarment. Scales may be enlarged to reduce working time.

either individual card scales or cutout bands of felt sewn to undergarment

flat topped tubular helms of thick card with felt strips glued over

surcoat over mail

thick card shape

felt →

card →

felt

Knight's helms

KNIGHT

Chain mail

Macramé, or knotting with yarns/cords →

metal washers

long laces or tape washers sewn to undergarment

front of leg mail with enclosed toe cap

washers sewn to undergarment

If a large quantity of washers is available, they will be very suitable but must each be stitched to the undergarment.

205

Chain mail, although still in use as a basic garment, was more and more often covered by various paddings and plates. Knights were guarded by protective plate from head to foot. Helmets developed to include visors. Knees and elbows had special armour pieces and feet and hands were covered by overlapping plates.

Weapons shown on pages 216 and 217.

fixed plate helmet-felt cap method, felt, card & buckram

hinged visor helmet

helm-see page 205

cord edging

string
gauntlet from old cycle glove: glue string round fingers, metal spray or paint

mail-see pages 204 and 205

2 KNIGHTS

Early plate armour was confined to knees, lower leg, elbows and lower arm

quilted jacket

CROSSBOWMAN

felt cap with felt under, or wire and papier mâché

wire pivot/hinge

visor

helmet construction as shown on previous pages - with addition of visor

Helmets with visor

glue mail to under side

206

1~ shaping armour within old nylon stocking/tights ~ glue allow to dry, cut nylon in gap and glue under

1

2

Leg plate armour

corrugated card, felt or thick card

A

2 ~ card or felt shaped round a cylinder ~ size or shellac ~ untie and trim when dry

straps glued and stapled inside ~ pass through slots

strengthen all pivot points with glued muslin or buckram

BACK VIEW OF LEFT LEG

A
B
C
D
E

long paper fasteners ~ ends bent over and cover in muslin inside

B

C

D

knee pieces ~ cut dart, glue and staple over, cover in muslin

glue card shapes

foot pieces for

E

15th cent. armour

thick elastic instep

Leather top jerkin

press studs as alternative to straps

felt or thick blanket or strong foam rubber ~ paint to simulate red leather

leather strap

thick felt or leather sword belt ~ bottle tops or scrap items for decoration

Arm plate armour

hollow for arm pit (also hollow out leg armour at groin)

thick elastic glued and stapled inside ~ straps as alternative

A

B

C

D

E

A

B

C

shoulder piece for 15th. cent. armour

thick elastic

E

D

LATE RENAISSANCE ARMOUR: 16th century (Elizabethan England)

This period shows the peak in the art of armour design. The body was completely covered by plate, with overlapping ribs over all mobile parts. Swords were large and heavy, helmets often crested.

parts built from felt or cut, shaped and hammered from thin aluminium sheet

optional thin crest

Weapons shown on pages 218 and 219.

The close helmet

visor

C

A B C

visor up- bevor down

helmet

bevor

plate armour completely covers figure

Ribbed armour

elastic and dowel toggle clips

Left: the complete helmet.

To put on a helmet, the head fits into the helmet and the bevor is lowered and clipped into position. The visor may be raised or lowered as required.

Other helmets

Kettle type– see also page 204

Sallet types

cut darts to shape and join, glue and sew

place foot in slipper-measure bands of felt, then tape along sides

cut out old slipper

Common soldiers continued to wear the helmets of earlier periods – the kettle type was popular in England but on the Continent of Europe the sallet types were preferred.

Footwear

Gauntlets

felt bands

use old leather or plastic cycling gauntlets for base

felt strips glue & staple ~ spray metallic paint

Armpiece

card base

felt/card strips glued over card base ~ staple ends

thick elastic tape

all parts sprayed/painted in metallic finish

felt or card strips over card base

simple method of simulating plates ~ use strings at regular intervals (see small inset above)

glue on string for 'fishtail'

hinges

ends of paper fastener turned out and covered in muslin or buckram

elastic instep

more subtle shaping can be achieved by cuts in material ~ open out and glue muslin over

Breastplate

either individual strips of felt overlapping ~ or cut from single piece and glue strings across to simulate plates

shape breastplate over dummy (see page 195) and shape out centre front to sharp edge ~ stiffen with shellac

sew on 'skirt' base to breastplate

cover ends with muslin

see page 207 for strap fixing

cord edging

wool, Macramé, etc., for 'mail' (see page 205)

Legpiece

Construction similar to that of Gothic armour on previous pages – differences lie mainly in more decorative finish on later armour.

209

17th CENTURY ARMOUR

English Civil War

Pikemen wore breast- and back-plates with wide skirt-like tassets and the morion helmet. Cavalrymen tended to wear lobstertail pot helmets. Musketeers and cavaliers often wore the gorget.

Weapons shown on pages 220 and 221.

Helmets

Morion

ostrich or other feathers
card crest
felt cap
small hollow tube - glue to back of crest
felt or card
two halves joined with tape and staples

Lobstertail

felt skull cap
thick card
heavy gauge wire
felt or card ear-flaps and 'tail'
pass wire guard through peak - bend over wires and cover in glued buckram

ARQUEBUSIER

with gun and gun-rest

gorget

finish all armour with metallic paint

lentils, etc. for rivets

Morion helmet - feathers can be omitted

shoulder straps to join breastplate if fitted at top - purely decorative if joined at sides by straps as shown here

string ribs

buff leather gloves

tasset

ribbons to match colour of tunic

common brown shoes - add thick bows

PIKEMAN

'lobstertail' helmet

buff leather coats

CAVALIER

the bridle gauntlet for left hand

Gorget

fix with press studs, strap or laces

pattern for gorget

Boots

card

BOOT

make boot-shoes by turning down Wellington tops - then insert card as shown - staple or stitch

paint as brown leather

felt strips on shoulder

breastplates built over dummy (see page 195)

leather belt

tasset - cut up centre to make two halves up to belt/waist level

felt

Pikeman's armour

Cavalryman's breastplate

leather 'tongues' to match boot

spurs built with heavy gauge wire

CAVALRYMAN

18th, 19th and 20th centuries

Armour was largely abandoned after the 17th century as new weaponry made it virtually useless. The 19th century saw a revival in armour for ceremonial occasions (the Household Cavalry in the British army, for example) but only to a limited degree for combat – the gorget to protect the neck, cuirass and helmets for cavalry.

For practical purposes, the military uniform of the 18th and 19th centuries was a full costume and it can be hired as a complete outfit.

20th century helmets can be obtained on hire through costume suppliers, local antique dealers or the enthusiastic collector of military paraphernalia.

GREEKS – Arms

Swords

plywood shape

shape swords as shown below

build up with felt, cord, metal scrap etc.

glue and screw

two wood sides for handle

secure strap with glue, wood strip and screws

plywood cutout (curve – see next page)

Spears – basically as Roman (see opposite page).

Shields

fiddle shaped shield

painted decoration

canvas/leather straps

wire frame, wire mesh and papier mâché construction

old refuse bin lid – handle disguised as hub by covering with papier mâché/pulp, etc. secure strap behind by drilling and fixing nuts and bolts

cut in armour for spear

frame of holder threaded through belt

end of 'spear' dowel clear to fit holder

leather strap/belt made to fit part of body concerned

old style mop holder – or hollow cylinder attached to metal frame

Device for spear sticking in a body

Shield construction

Shields for all periods are easily made from a pliable board such as hardboard or thin (skin) plywood. If a deep curve is required, steam the board and allow to dry between two fixed points to mould into shape (see diagram opposite). Wood formers or straps should fit within the curve and be glued and tacked into position.

softwood shape – dimensions dependent on type and period

plane sides approx. 15° from centre line

thin sheet aluminium – fold to shape & tack at centre

screw together

1 cut back handle

2

glued cord or string **3**

Sword construction

The basic shape for Greek and Roman swords is made from softwood. Plane to the correct angle and build hilt across shaft as shown in (**2**). Cover with thin sheet alloy; glue on metal foil; or paint with metallic colours if realism is required.

ROMANS – Arms

Shields

felt cutout decoration scrap metal

basic shape after setting curve (see below)

shield arm support ~ cut to fit curve

thick felt edging ~ studs/rivets of seeds, cereals etc.,

battens screwed to board (or old wood floor)

hardboard/plywood, soaked and shaped between two fixed battens

Lathe turned spear head

hardboard/plywood cutouts ~ add pulp and wood strips for relief effects

dowel

string

S·P·Q·R

scrap odd-ments

25 mm dowel (or 25 × 25 mm section ~ round off handle)

half coconut or papier mâché

dowel

felt strips

nail or screw support

two halves taped

tapes glued inside shell

dowel

Standards and spears

All pole-like weapons and standards are constructed on a suitable length of dowel rod or broom handle (25 mm to 35 mm diameter). Spear heads are formed of carved wood pieces drilled to take the shaft – or the dowel can be spliced and the blade fitted inside. Larger heads are built of two or more pieces of thin plywood, bound with wire and shaped to a point. Decorative pieces on standards can be of wood and board with paper pulp modelling. Gild with metallic colours (see page III).

scabbard fixed into belt by leather or felt strip ~ glue and staple (or sew)

Scabbards

Scabbards should be slightly longer than the dagger or sword – see page 216 for the method of construction.

213

ARMS: 11th and 12th century (Norman)

The chief weapon during this period was the sword. It differed little from earlier types except for the more elaborate hilt. However, it was probably during the 12th century that the greatest of English medieval weapons was developed – the longbow (see opposite).

Swords

thick tape or cord

Norman shields

shield lengths approx. 120 cm.

cross guard of plywood

shaped blade ~ see page 212 ~ with sheet metal tacked on top

hilt slightly tapered

pommel of carved wood or built of pulp and wire ~ secure with long screw

arm support of webbing, leather or thick rubber ~ secure between shield and edging with glue and screws.

plywood or hardboard shape

a simple sword support can be made: stitching a loop into a strap ~ or fixing a wood block as shown here ~ cut from one piece if preferred.

typical sword shapes of the period ~

approx. 50 mm wide edging of thin wood strip or plywood to strengthen

decorations may be painted only, or built up with scrap materials first and then painted.

cross section of shield

cut tape after pulling tight

Longbows

Bows that require stretching on stage need to be flexible and should be made of ash. Those used purely as decoration can be made in any softwood.

approx. 1½ metre softwood strip 50×16mm. showing planed shape and end extensions

plywood/wood pieces, planed and glued together

finish shape with spoke shave

glue and screw 16mm wood strips to thicken centre

glue and bind with thick tape or cord

thick string knot/tie to end

An early crossbow

plywood

thin dowel for bolt

mortice and tenon joint

build bow as above (but smaller)

nylon cord

tie rope round bow & shaft over tenon joint

sawn slot

Axes

shape from heavy gauge wire or metal scrap

collar to fit dowel.

card sides to blend collar into axe head

shaft of 50×50 mm. softwood

plywood head

thick dowel

Arrows and quivers

approx. 50 mm. decorated felt strips ~ top and bottom

position of 'false' arrows (flights only) in board

glue and tack strap to quiver

cut feathers thru' centre and glue shaped pieces to dowel sides

slightly taper sides ~ cut from thin plywood or hardboard

flights only set in board

tapered from 75×16 mm softwood

5/6 mm dowel

215

ARMS: Gothic period, 13th – 14th centuries

During this period the sword developed into a longer heavier weapon. Axes and maces (metal-headed clubs) became more popular.

See page 221 for making blades.

Swords

assorted string, wires and tapes

13th century swords show little change in blades except for the falchion (left) and sometimes a longer hilt (see above).

Variations on crossguard shape

wood or metal

14th century blades were longer. They had a tall tapering hilt and often a large pommel.

Scabbards

Scabbards will hang correctly if the belt is attached as shown – this gives the characteristic slope to swords and daggers when worn. Cardboard is an ideal material for scabbards.

Plywood blade – cover in foil, thin sheet metal or metallic paint

decorate either in relief with string, sequins, etc. and paint – or paint or spray in metallic and other colours

tab glued to other side

thick card or strawboard scabbard pattern

staple end of scabbard and finish with shaped band of felt – glue, trim and paint

metal oddments on thick wooden disc, screw to handle with coach screw

either paint, or bind in wire, string etc.

carved wood ~ metal finish

14th cent. more tapered

216

Other arms

Maces

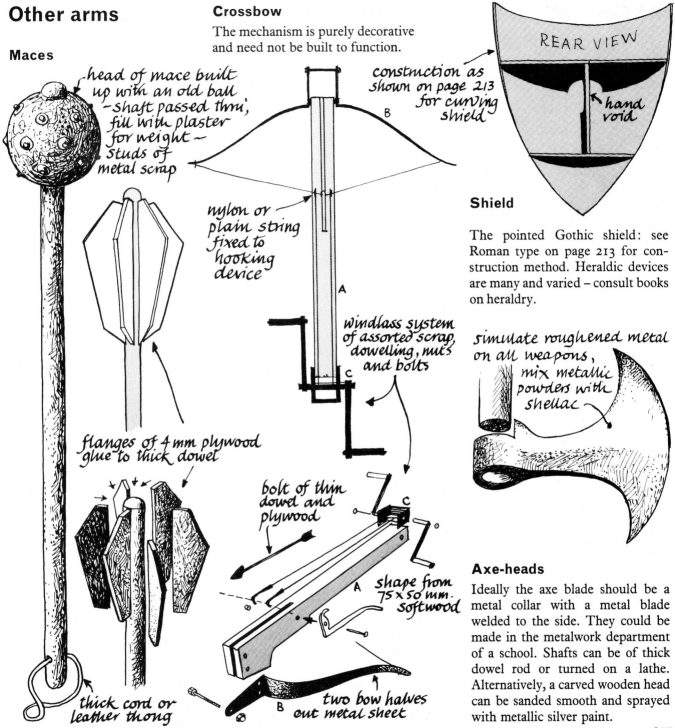

head of mace built up with an old ball – shaft passed thru', fill with plaster for weight – studs of metal scrap

flanges of 4 mm plywood glue to thick dowel

thick cord or leather thong

Crossbow

The mechanism is purely decorative and need not be built to function.

construction as shown on page 213 for curving shield

B

nylon or plain string fixed to hooking device

A

C

windlass system of assorted scrap, dowelling, nuts and bolts

bolt of thin dowel and plywood

A

C

shape from 75 x 50 mm. softwood

B

two bow halves cut metal sheet

Shield

REAR VIEW

hand void

The pointed Gothic shield: see Roman type on page 213 for construction method. Heraldic devices are many and varied – consult books on heraldry.

simulate roughened metal on all weapons, mix metallic powders with shellac

Axe-heads

Ideally the axe blade should be a metal collar with a metal blade welded to the side. They could be made in the metalwork department of a school. Shafts can be of thick dowel rod or turned on a lathe. Alternatively, a carved wooden head can be sanded smooth and sprayed with metallic silver paint.

217

ARMS: Renaissance and Elizabethan, 15th – 16th centuries

coach screw, pulp and cord

coach screw

turned wood or pulp handle

heavy gauge wire

assorted finishes — painted wood, foil or thin sheet metal

felt

blade

Swords

These drawings show the evolution of the knucklebow (which was to lead eventually to the enclosed cup-hilts of the 17th and 18th centuries) from simple curved and looped bars (left) to the curving of the hilt towards the pommel.

The hilt, pommel and looped bars can all be built round a coach bolt or large screw attached to the 'blade' – the hilt can be part of the blade if of sufficient girth, but a bolt or screw drilled through will give added strength.

(See page 221 for basic blade shaping.)

Daggers (all periods)

Daggers (in effect miniature swords) are made in the same way as swords. The scabbards tend to be more elaborate in both ornament and colour. Hilts can be enriched with nail heads, 'jewels', etc.

painted decoration

Quillon dagger

Scabbard for a dagger

basic construction as shown on page 216 to fit appropriate dagger length

basic shape from 30×10 mm. softwood or plywood

two parts 3/4 mm. plywood – glue and screw

wood, felt pieces – glued and tack

Roundel dagger

nail/tack studding

plywood discs

1

2

either shape from dowel (1) or from 3/4 mm plywood or softwood (2)

pipette taped against dagger

thumb should reach bulb when hand grips handle

Device for making bloody cut

See also *Blood* on page 263 of the section on make-up.

16th. cent. halberd blade shapes of 3/4 mm plywood.

metal finish

metal finish ~ wood finish

Halberds/pikes

Popular weapons during this period for foot soldiers. The blade is best fitted into a split in the dowel.

sandpaper edges to thin knife-edge metallic finish

1

2

screw

felt

1 - slot through
2 - slot down

War hammers

Used mainly by horsemen as an armour-penetrating weapon.

Old hammer head ~ or carved, turned wood

cut sheet metal or carved wood

plywood disc & large nail head (pulp or metal)

30 x 30 mm shaped shaft meccano strips

Cross-taped

plywood flanges ~ top ornaments of turned/carved wood; felt and pulp or scrap metal oddments

Mace

22/25 mm. dowel shaft

thin plywood discs

tape or cord hand grip

collars of felt or cord

paint shafts in strong dark gloss colours

spiral cord around shaft - glue & tack

Spear

plywood blade ~ set in shaft of approx. 50 mm. dowel ~ see illustration below right

6/9 mm dowel

Crossbow

see also pages 215 and 217 for change in shape of cross-bows

Boar spear

stop-bar of thin dowel

ARMS: 17th century (English Civil War)

Rapier

The rapier is a long, thin two-edged blade sword for quick cut-and-thrust action. Note how the hilt has evolved into a cupped shape from the earlier knucklebow type. See opposite for the making of blades.

Broadsword

glued cord

pulped paper pommel over wire and screw

fill between wires with tape or taped card

cup shape ~ half coconut; papier mâché on wire mesh; old plastic ball, etc.

wooden blocks or beads ~ secured with coach screw

double & twisted heavy gauge wire

thick felt

string details

metal/plastic scrap details on pommel

optional ornament - cut card, felt and string - finish in metallic colours

paper pulp knob over wire

assorted knucklebows on broadswords: wire frame, felt or tape wrapped round to attain required thickness ~ shellac and paint

details of pulp and/or paint

Cup-hilted rapier

curved cross-guard in two halves — glue, screw and tape across gaps

Quillon dagger

The broadsword was used by the cavalry. The blade is wide, 50–75 mm. Hilts can be very elaborate with three or four bars joining the pommel.

See pages 222–224 for guns of all periods.

Pole-arms or pikes

Pole-arms are now more decorative and used mainly for ceremonial purposes.

optional decoration – fibre tip pen on metallic background colour

3/4 mm plywood

tie ribbons round pole with adhesive tape or glued felt

add collars after fixing blade to pole

25 mm to 50 mm dowel

alternative ways of securing blade to poles:
above: slot at top
below: slot in side

3/4 mm plywood blade-sandpaper down edges, paint in metallic colour add decoration in fibre tip or paint (see above)

pole lengths between 1½ and 2 metres

plane angle from centre line

drawn centre line

bench stop

chisel out handle shape

Making sword blades

Secure a length of wood in a vice or with clamps. Draw a centre line lengthwise down each side of the wood and plane out the slope and angle of the blade.

221

GUNS: all periods

All the guns shown on these pages are for purely decorative, non-functioning purposes. None is made to fire – only a pivot on the trigger of the flintlock is introduced if required.

If the detailed making seems too elaborate, an alternative is to purchase some of the many excellent reproductions available (they may have to be 'toned down' from a very new shiny look).

If firing is necessary, an antique casing (from those shown here) can be built round a starting pistol.

Construction of basic parts, as shown right, can be adapted to any of the guns illustrated.

Hand gun (14th century)

The hand gun is in effect a small cannon attached to a pole.

wood or metal 'hook'

stock or pole

chisel out slot

gun

metal/wood disc

bronzed finish all parts of gun

thick dowel pole

plane and chisel from wood block

Matchlock (15th century)

The lever can be of heavy-gauge wire thickened at the pivot with sheet tin soldered to the wire.

cut out slot

screw pivot

large bamboo for cannon

bands of string, cord or wire

pivoted lever for match – cut from sheet metal or use existing iron bar/rod

'match'

long wood pole (the stock) – use thick dowel

cannon

finish cannon & lever in bronze

Matchlock (16th century)

stock – simulate weathered wood

barrel of scrap metal tube or dowel

webbing strap

mechanical details of scrap metal

cut sheet tin

saw and carve from softwood block

**Wheel-lock
(mid 16th century)**

barrel cut from sheet aluminium or thick card, stiffened with shellac ~ finish with metallic colours

STOCK

ramrod (see below)

flair out with pulp, cord or cut sheet metal

reverse side

approx. 25 cm

wood base, sheet metal & scrap oddments for details

lock and trigger from scrap and sheet metal

carve stock from softwood

approx. 75 cm

old golf ball or similar size object

screw through to stock

Blunderbuss (mid 18th century)

approx. 40 cm

softwood barrel plane out angles

authenticity:-
reference should be made to appropriate gun books for accurate dimension and detail

plastic or rubber tube

ramrod of 4mm dowel or metal rod

metal & wire

stock — carve from softwood punched texture or painted decoration

13 cm

either cut from block of polystyrene or shape from thick felt

trigger and guard of cut sheet aluminium or tin

flintlock — cut sheet metal - ornament/decoration can be omitted

**Pistol flask
(mid 19th century)**

18th century flintlock – method of construction

Musket (17th–19th centuries)

felt, cord or metal bands

metal tube or dowel

total length of 140 cm (approx.)

carved wood stock
(see previous pages)

thick dowel

Gun rest

wire or wood

gun-rest in use

approx. 21 cm

**Pepperbox
revolver, c. 1800**

An example of the many multi-barrelled small guns of the late 18th and early 19th centuries.

large metal tube
suitable to receive
girth of barrels

either shape barrels
from approx. 35 mm
dowel or build up set of
six 12 mm dowels or
metal tubes

carved wood
stock

**Colt revolver
(mid 19th century)**

The most famous of all revolvers – for more detailed information on the different calibres of Colt revolvers it will be useful to consult the many good reference books on the subject.

construct revolver as other weapons on
these pages — or preferably use one of
many scale plastic models available
today

Costume accessories 9

CROWNS · OCCUPATIONAL ACCESSORIES · PAPER
PULP AND MOULDS · JEWELLERY

CROWNS – 1: a basic design and some construction methods

Materials

1 Cut shapes of stiff cartridge paper, stencil paper, felt or similar flexible material. **2** Scrap metals, buttons, beads, springs, etc. **3** Cord and string. **4** Muslin and scrim. **5** Pulp and paper. **6** Tissue paper and torn newsprint. **7** Stapler. **8** Adhesives, scissors, knife. **9** Light and medium gauge wire. **10** Felt pieces. **11** Paint.

Assembly

Staple or stitch basic parts together, glueing all surfaces *before* fixing.

Building up of structure

Glue cord to outer edges and cover with pasted tissues, tapping them gently into crevices with a brush. Strengthen with layers of papier mâché and muslin. Leave to dry and then shellac.

Decorating

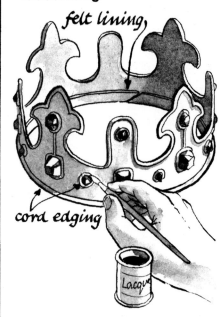

Use coloured foil or sweet wrappers and bright enamels for the jewels. Paint the rest with metal powders in shellac.

Felt method

circumference of head

Cut out a paper pattern, the circumference determined by the actor's head + 2 cm flaps.

Lay out on felt or similar material stiffened with shellac. Chalk round the pattern and cut out. Use leftover pieces for decorations.

felt decorations

Stitch or staple the flaps together. Bend the crown to the required shape before the shellac hardens.

Jewels are small cut pieces of felt covered with foil or paint. Metal paints and powders can be applied to the whole crown with a brush or spraygun.

Felt cap method

Steam an old felt hat (see helmet-making on page 197) to the right size. Cut round with scissors to give a smooth edge.

Staple or stitch a 5 cm rim outside the cap. Shellac both parts.

stapling band

Build up the crown over the cap, with strips across and a centre bob.

Try variations on string decorations.

Wire method

A strip of card or paper is wrapped round the actor's head to get the right circumference.

staple

medium gauge wire frame

fine wire mesh

taped wire

A wire frame is built round the paper pattern ring – the paper is later removed. Tie wires as shown on page 233.

paper pulp jewels

Paper mâché is pasted over the wire mesh (approximately 4 layers). The decorative parts are added with more pulp or felt. Apply a coat of shellac, then a coat of paint, then another coat of shellac. Finish with metal powders, etc. See notes on page 111.

felt band and decorations

227

CROWNS – 2

Fabric over frame – traditional crown

fabric

slope of frame may be in or out – as below.

card rim glued to frame

cord edging

Drape fabric over wire frame and tuck under top ring.

Ornament with metal scrap, paste jewellery, beads, etc. Enamel and gild with metal powder in shellac or P.V.A. medium.

Tall cylindrical crown

A tall cylinder with a slight cone shape can be constructed from stiff card or from felt stiffened with shellac.

Finish decoration with cut felt pieces soaked in shellac or size. Spray or paint with metallic paints – or with metal powders in shellac or P.V.A. medium.

tape and staple

wide band of thick felt

felt pieces glued to card cylinder

decorations of cut felt or paper pulp – lacquer for jewels

Ornate Eastern crown

Assemble as shown. Staple tabs. Decorate with strings, cords and felts. Paint with gold metal paint.

A

B   C

assemble parts A, B and C as shown

felt pieces

string/cord decorations

Other shapes

staple

paper fastener 'rivets'

Using similar methods, a simple ring type with four plain points can be constructed. 'Rivets' are featured as the only ornament.

Any of the materials already mentioned would be suitable for this tall, pointed, 'wizard' style crown.

fine wire mesh

papier mâché

Unusual shapes can be constructed with wire, wire mesh and papier mâché.

Coronets

Coronets are more delicate than crowns and need fine detail on the top edge. Interesting spaces can be created by adding raised parts to the top edge.

Variety can be achieved by the use of various scrap items – feathers, beads, etc.

This illustration shows a ring of felt surmounted by feathers, combs, sticks, hat-pins and scrap metal, all secured by fine wire.

felt band *wire or shellac string*

cut metal, beads, etc.

Tiered crowns

card disc glued inside top

string pattern

shorter version

bands of felt or card

Tall Biblical crowns can be made from simple cones of card, as shown above.

Bishop's mitre

sequins beads, etc for decoration

glue two halves inside band

The mitre requires two halves bound at the bottom by a band, with two 'tassels' attached.

Greek/Roman sandals

buckram or felt sewn to sock

Footwear

Simple footwear can be constructed over canvas shoes, old shoes and rubber boots. Old shoe soles and shoe socks can have tapes and felt glued and stapled underneath.

cords or leather thongs threaded through boot socks

high tongue of stiffened felt

plimsoll with felt over ~ stitched to sole

plimsoll

shoe

17th cent. shoe

14th cent. shoe

card and silver paper

18th cent. buckled shoe

stitch thick white blanket/felt etc.

shoes ~elastic sided type

19th cent. riding boot

wellington top turned down and felt rim glued or stitched to low edge

17th cent. boot shoe

OCCUPATIONAL COSTUME ACCESSORIES

Certain plays and musicals demand accessories relating to particular occupations often of an early period. The musical 'Oliver', for example, requires various street traders: strawberry sellers, a knife grinder, a milkmaid, etc. Costumes for such trades are beyond the scope of this book but a few items illustrated on these two pages can be useful and are not difficult to make.

Milkmaid's yoke and pail

heavy gauge wire frame
wire mesh
wood or metal strip under for strength
papier mâché
leather strap
ladle
tin can - rivetted metal strip
pails built over bucket in thick card or plywood - or construct entirely in plywood and wire for handle
thick felt

A yoke and early wooden pail (17th century). Pail can be fixed to yoke or carried on the head.

Postman's caps

felt shape - slight slope at back
white card badges
wide top
card peaks
black gloss finish
tape band

The double-peaked postman's cap (1904) can be made from an existing cap with peaks added.

Sweep's brush and cap

sticks of 25mm dowel or bamboo - paint all black
small straps
old broom bristles - or make from strips of black paper
glue and paint as brass or tin plate
stitch tabs to inside of cap - turn side up and stitch on to side
thick felt

The sweep's brush is shown in a closed position.

The sweeps' fantail hat was also used by dustmen in the 1800s.

Chef's hat

white starched cotton - pleat and glue/sew to inside of card band

Chef's hat of the 19th century. The band gradually became deeper to reach the height seen today.

Carpenter's tools and paper cap

double-handed saw handles in two halves – screw blade between

cords

saw blade & square in thin plywood

shape tool bag from sack or large piece of felt

build hat from paper square

The paper cap was common to many trades in the 19th century but was associated chiefly with carpenters. The paper-folding method is complicated but can be found in most **origami** books.

Stove-pipe hat

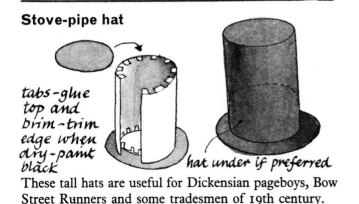

tabs – glue top and brim – trim edge when dry – paint black

hat under if preferred

These tall hats are useful for Dickensian pageboys, Bow Street Runners and some tradesmen of 19th century.

Hawker's tray

thick cane handle

tape strap for shoulders →

trays – wicker type or make from plywood and paint as wicker work

Early police and fireman's helmets

← small crest of card

paper pulp over wire and/or card

felt strap – paint gold finish

chin strap of tape

These helmets can be constructed as Roman helmets – see page 202.

Water seller's tankard

old coal hod or construct from thin plywood –

bands of stiffened felt (shellac)

spout built over tube and wire mesh – papier mâché

paint lines and colour to simulate planking

taped double heavy gauge wire handle

FANS

Ostrich fan

(see page 166 for these props in a setting)

Mesopotamian fan

groups of goose feathers as alternative to ostrich feathers

thick felt

hardboard or thin plywood

25 mm dowel

cord bands

bottle tops secured with paper fasteners

broaden handle with thick felt and cords

plywood or hardboard backing

curved card

wood blocks with holes to secure feathers

sun motif of felt

1 to 1½ metres in height

build up shape with maché to blend dowel with top of fan

thick dowel

wood disc

pulp over end of screw

thick cord bands

handle widened with band of felt

heavy gauge wire

wood disc and pulp or metal knob

simple folding fans - score and fold alternative sides and secure at end or cut separate strips and fix wire one end and tape at open end

tape

paint bands or floral decoration before folding

Folding fans

glue on stiff card strip

SPECTACLES, etc.

Do not fit any glass.

thread round ends

square shape-fine gauge wire

Square spectacles

method of taping wire

Monocle

twist wire to form hole for cord

Pince-nez

thin black tapes or cords

If pairs of spectacles are available through antique dealers, etc. they would be preferable if very exact standards are required. The items shown here are adequate for school productions.

PURSES and POMANDERS

cords to belt

felt or leather — thread belt through

Medieval pouch and purse

strap over belt

press button

15th–17th century purses

chain

felt or leather strap

Pomanders
old tennis or rubber balls with glued felt strips and sequins, etc. for ornaments

long cords with tassel

thin leather strip

two sides of felt stiffened with shellac ~ paint decorations

black silk or dyed cotton

beads

tassells

19th century handbags

JEWELLERY and ORNAMENTS

Jewellery, medallions, chains of office and all small and decorative parts of costume, armour and properties can be made from plaster, pulp and scrap materials.

Smaller items can be repeated many times from a common mould. Illustrated here are methods of making the pulp and the moulds.

Making fine paper pulp

You will need plenty of newspapers, sugar paper and a small quantity of caustic potash to assist the breaking down of paper fibres during boiling.

Cover with water and boil in a large metal bucket, making sufficient pulp to meet your needs over a period of time – it can be stored. Keep on the boil for some hours, beating and thumping occasionally with a squared piece of timber to make a fine pulp. Add water if too dry.

Cleanse the pulp thoroughly in cold water – a wide piece of butter-muslin is ideal for draining and then squeezing out surplus water.

Remove or rub down all remaining lumps. Add one tenth (by volume) of paste and one tenth of plaster or whiting as a filler, enough to make a pliable pulp with a clay-like consistency.

For storage, pack in air-tight tins.

Making a mould

Draw a design on paper and then model it in clay or plasticine. Make it about 10–15 mm thick.

Be careful to avoid any undercuts which would prevent the finished 'positive' design being removed from the mould.

Prepare your working surface with newspaper. Place a 3 cm card strip round the design and join with sticky tape. Seal off gaps underneath with clay or plasticine.

Sift plaster through the fingers into a cup or small bowl about a third full of water. Continue until the plaster appears just above the surface of the water. Stir gently with the fingers until all lumps and air bubbles have been removed.

Pour the prepared plaster inside the card circle until it reaches the top edge. Any leftover plaster should be used immediately on other prepared moulds.

When the plaster has set turn the mould over and carefully prise out the original model, taking care not to damage the plaster.

Thoroughly clean out all traces of clay or plasticine. Use a stiff brush (hog bristle will do) to work oil or Vaseline into all parts of the 'negative' mould. It is usual to leave the plaster for a few days to dry out, but it can be used immediately if time is pressing.

Using the prepared paper pulp, press a sufficient quantity into the greased mould. Flatten off with a straight-edge, pulled across at an angle.

Leave for some hours before removing the 'positive' design from the mould. If it sticks, prise gently around the edges – check that no undercuts are preventing the pulp cast from coming clear.

Using moulds

Should a large number of ornaments be needed, multiple moulds can be prepared. Sets of moulds of approximately the same size and design can be placed closely together inside the card frame before pouring in the plaster. The illustrations on this page show examples – and the photograph on the facing page shows a chain made up of the 'positive' shapes from these moulds.

Right: Two illustrations showing the ornaments used on armour and helmets. The small squares over the shoulder piece and the oblongs on the lower edge were pressed out of the moulds below.

Bases and supports for jewellery

Large items of jewellery such as collars or heavy medallions are best built up on a plywood, hardboard or felt base. If in felt, stiffen first with shellac or P.V.A. medium.

Collars

shell collar of limpets and periwinkles —inverted limpets on inner band

felt base and central ring

felt base and decorations with buttons

seeds or lentils as background

bottle tops, beads and felt discs on felt base

metallic powders and shellac finish

Collars require large bold designs. Experiment with all kinds of scrap materials: metal scrap, wire, felt, cord, pieces of plastic, etc. All can be securely fixed with P.V.A. adhesive or Evo-Resin W.

Chains and pendants

Above: chain of office or chain with pendant. Each piece is firmly glued to a narrow finger bandage or, if preferred, to a thin, strong tape. A staple can be carefully driven into the back of each piece through the fabric.

Pendants on a golden or silver chain. The chain can be built around a medium-gauge wire with small beads, etc. threaded on to the wire and glued in position – spaced out as required.

alternative pendants for bead necklace→

card base string

card cutouts and beads

suspender clips and hair grips

beads→

Various kinds of jewellery

Necklaces

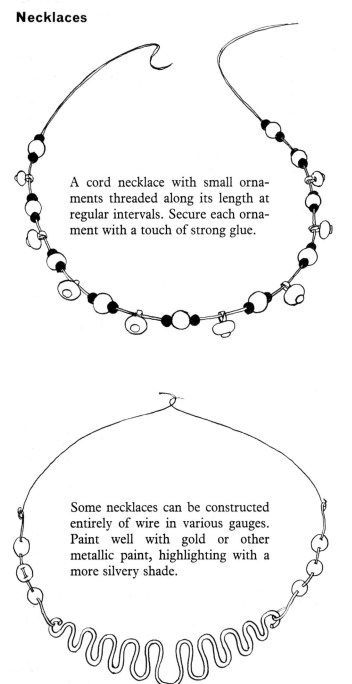

A cord necklace with small ornaments threaded along its length at regular intervals. Secure each ornament with a touch of strong glue.

Some necklaces can be constructed entirely of wire in various gauges. Paint well with gold or other metallic paint, highlighting with a more silvery shade.

cord and string

large and small washers

bracelet cut from aluminium sheet (smooth out all edges)

glued tape hinge

strips of cut felt on card cylinder

felt bracelet built from two halves – method shown below

clear Shellac

small can – wood blocks for stability

Bracelets can be made in two halves: each half is moulded over a tin can, with felt soaked in shellac. The two halves can then be overlapped and clipped together with press studs, at one side, and hinged on the other with glued tape.

Alternatively, make a cardboard roll slightly wider than the wrist in order to slip over the hand.

In either case, the bracelets can be decorated in ways previously described, appropriate to the historical period.

Brooches

Brooches can either be pressed out of moulds or built up from wire (soldered or tied), seeds or cereals.

Another method: use a small base and glue to it small beads, etc. surrounded by metal strips in a sun-ray effect.

seeds and cereals

Girdles, with buckles, clasp, etc.

alternative ornament ~use curtain rings

ordinary buckle concealed behind large button, etc.

bottle tops and felt pieces

clasp similar to Scout's type or clasp of thick wire

felt strips or matches

limpet or other shells

Use an existing belt and mount various ornaments along the entire length, leaving gaps if desired. Secure with P.V.A. medium – leave to dry thoroughly.

Buttons

These can be made as brooches, but with holes for threading. Or they can be existing large buttons decorated with added scraps.

macaroni glued to card base

washers

thick cards

card bases

string patterns

Rings and earrings

Make rings by twisting strands of medium-gauge wire round the finger – tie into knot and build up with pulp. Cheap paste jewellery can also be used.

piece of metal tubing

paper pulp over wire tie

linked rings

beads

Earrings can also be made of wire. Allow separate joints for a swinging effect.

large bauble glued to pin

head of plastic wood

squiggles of glue on card base

metal pieces glued into ball of plastic wood

Pins Use an existing pin if available, building up the end with wire and other scrap.

Decorate all jewellery with metal paints or metal powders in glue size, shellac or P.V.A. medium.

ITEMS FOR A SCHOOL NATIVITY PLAY

Nativity plays require little or no scenery – perhaps a hint at a stable or, preferably, a cave-like dwelling. The properties required are described below.

A simple crib

blockboard or plywood ends – hardboard or thin plywood sides

straw

crib complete as box or with cross legs of 75 x 25 mm softwood

halving joint on legs

Angels' wings

For lengthening the wings, hold a stick in each hand and drape materials (cloth with feather shapes attached looks effective) over the stick.

concealed stick

More traditional wings: use a wire frame attached to straps to tie across the chest.

'feathers' glued to canvas

wire frame – cover with light canvas, etc.

tapes

Build up wire frames for the wings themselves and cover with fabric stretched tightly. Attach 'feathers' if desired.

Shepherds' crooks

Use a 25 mm dowel or bamboo stick; insert heavy-gauge wire at one end.

tape dowel to wire

heavy gauge wire

25 mm dowel

pad out with paper pulp

Wrap a padding of paper round the wire where it meets the dowel or bamboo, narrowing as you work towards the tip of the wire. Finish with self-adhesive tape and paint.

Primary school Nativity Play: note the use of simple sheeting for angels at the sides.

The gifts

Look at pages 160–163 for examples of various pots and page 168 for boxes. The important thing is to aim at variety of shape, the decoration can be quite simple.

Here are shown a sphere, an oblong box and a chalice-like shape. Many other possibilities can be tried – but differences in shape should be obvious from a distance.

casket shape from plywood or cardboard

spherical shape built around ball

chalice shape – cotton reels and wood discs

Crowns

See pages 226–229 for method of construction.

Crowns can be elaborate or very simple but variety of shape is important as it is for the gifts. Here are three basic shapes:

cone and ring of stiff card

'velvet' inside

decorative cake band on card

A star

Make a wire frame, stretch tissue paper over it and place a lamp behind; alternatively, cover wire or card with silver foil.

paper star – score and fold

wire frame – tissue covered lamp and battery behind

ITEMS FOR A SCHOOL PASSION PLAY

Passion plays can be most effective if performed in the open, weather permitting. It is rewarding to work with large crowd movements in a natural environment.

The essential items for a Passion play are: Three crosses; Pilate's throne; Roman arms and armour; and small props – a crown of thorns, a bowl for washing and some stage blood. A stretcher will be useful if Christ is to be carried away.

A simple form of Roman armour is shown below:

1 Cut four lengths of card 5 cm wide, long enough to encircle the waist.

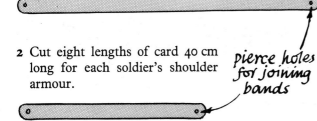

pierce holes for joining bands

2 Cut eight lengths of card 40 cm long for each soldier's shoulder armour.

3 Cover each card strip with thin foil, glueing it on with P.V.A. medium and folding the surplus foil to the back of each strip – one side only need be smooth.

fold over and glue metal foil

4 Each set of shoulder strips can be curved together and stapled, then sewn to the garment.

The waistband is secured at the front by lacing or press studs.

any convenient fasteners, press studs, etc....

secure with paper fasteners or tapes

Helmets and body armour are shown on pages 202–203, arms on page 213. (continued on next page)

Items for a passion play (continued)

The crosses

Ensure that they are strong in structure to carry the weight of actors. Cut lengths of timber and assemble as shown. Allow extra length for the depth of the hole. The Christus figure should be raised into position from the ground so it is important to place the cross base conveniently close to the hole. Ropes can effectively be used to pull the cross into a vertical positon. A wedge can be inserted at the rear of the cross to prevent movement.

Christus figure on Cross – rehearsal for an outdoor Passion play.

door/cupboard handles for hand supports

feet support – plywood side bracing

200 × 25 m front and back

75 mm plywood or hardboard

Thieves' crosses can be in form of a 'T'

30 cm extra length for depth of hole

ends – 200 × 75 m m softwood or thick plywood

BASE OF CROSS

wedge

hole – remove turf, dig hole and fit wood surround – allow 10° slope at rear for easy entry of cross – replace turf.

Throne

A throne suitable for a Passion play is shown on page 150.

A crown of thorns

Use either medium gauge wire or light ash twigs as a base – intertwine suitable twigs with this base.

Make-up and masks 10

MATERIALS · CHARACTER CREATION · AGEING · ETHNIC FACES · MASKS

BASIC REQUIREMENTS

The most basic requirements for applying make-up are a good mirror, a table in front of it for the make-up, a comfortable chair for the actor and as much light as you can possibly get. An actor sitting comfortably means a better result.

Make-up materials
Basic kit

- Box to contain make-up. Plastic tool or fishing tackle boxes are ideal, being cheap and readily available.
- Foundations. For amateur and student productions water-based cakes and Aquacolors are quick and easy to apply and can be used for face and body make-up.
- Cream liners for shading and eyeshadow. These are called Supracolors.
- Paintstick for highlighting very pale faces and greying small areas of hair.
- Translucent loose face powder. You only need the one colour for every skin tone (see colour list).
- Eyebrow pencil or cake eyeliner.
- Mascara (usually for females only).
- Blusher and a blusher brush.
- Brown powder shadow (females).
- Good quality eyeliner, lip and shading brushes.
- Lipsticks (females).
- Cosmetic sponge, cotton wool, cleanser and toning lotion.

Colour list

Kryolan range available world-wide.

White males

Foundation 6W or 7W Cake or Aquacolor
Highlight – 1W Supracolor
Powder – translucent TL3
Pencil – dark brown
Blusher – TC2
Lips – nothing unless very pale, then use a little EF9
Supracolor applied with a finger

Tanned and dark skins

Foundation – if necessary match to skin tone
Highlight – GG Supracolor or Chinese
Powder – translucent TL3
Pencil – dark brown or black
Blusher – T1
Lips – as above

White females

Foundation – 3W (fair skin) or 5W (deeper)
  Aquacolor or cream type
Highlight – 1W paintstick
Shading – mid-brown powder shadow
Eyeshadow – Supracolor 073 (soft grey-green)
Eyeliner/eyebrows – dark brown pencil or liner
Socket shadow – mid-brown powder shadow
Mascara – brownish black or black
Lipsticks – soft red, peach tone
Blusher – 075

Tanned and dark skins

Foundation – to match skin tone
Highlight – GG Supracolor or paintstick. Chinese for
  very dark skins
Shading – dark brown powder shadow
Powder – translucent TL3
Eyeliner/eyebrows – brownish black or black
Eyeshadow – Supracolor 483 (lilac)
Socket shadow – dark brown powder shadow
Blusher – T1
Lipstick – deep clear red

Apply foundation in broad strokes and then blend evenly.

Make-up is an art. Practise and experiment on yourself or others to achieve the effects you desire. You do not want a mask but a make-up that reflects and searches out the character being played.

Think first of the character and then look at the face, considering the structure, cheekbones, shape of nose, brow, jawline – then decide how to use the features to visually create the part to be acted.

STRAIGHT MAKE-UP FOR MALE AND FEMALE

The term 'straight make-up' means 'basic make-up'.

To prepare the skin and remove moisture or stickiness, pat skin tonic over the face before beginning. Avoid moisturiser under stage make-up, especially water-based types.

Male

Male make-up should always be subtle to look completely natural on stage. In small theatres the only requirement may be foundation to give the skin a healthy appearance. Cake make-up or Aquacolor is the ideal foundation for male faces as it is easy to apply and removable with soap and water.

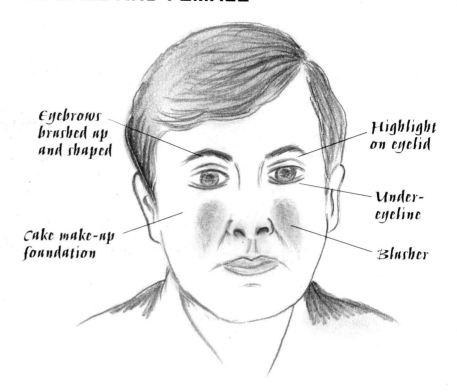

Eyebrows brushed up and shaped

Highlight on eyelid

Cake make-up foundation

Under-eyeline

Blusher

1 Using a wet cosmetic sponge, apply strokes of colour quickly across the forehead, down the nose, on each cheek and over the chin. Squeeze the sponge out and quickly blend the make-up evenly over the face. Take up a little more and apply to eyelids and the skin under them, ears and down the neck a little. Add extra to any ruddy areas. When the skin looks healthy, pat dry with a tissue.

2 The eyes will appear larger if highlight is used to pale the eyelids. It should look pale but not white. The same colour can be used to cover any small blemishes on the face.

3 Powder the eyelids with translucent powder to set the highlight and the rest of the face if it appears shiny. Generally cake make-up requires little powder unless cream highlights or shaders are used as well.

4 Apply dry rouge or blusher in a long triangular shape close to the nose with a brush. Avoid very large brushes which make it difficult to be accurate shapewise.

5 Define the eye by drawing a fine line under the lower lashes. This line does not go up to the corners or extend. Depending on the hair colour, dark brown or black should be chosen. Top eyelines are only necessary for very fair men or if a very dark wig is worn. Mascara is used only for fair lashes.

6 To enlarge the mouth, increase the size with a neutral-coloured lip pencil and soften with a fingertip. Mouths are only made up if they need more natural colour or enlarging. Use a little Kryolan EF9 Supracolor on a fingertip and blend it over the lips carefully. This is a strong colour and a tiny amount goes a long way.

7 Brush through the eyebrows with a damp toothbrush and if necessary add more colour using block mascara. Work against the natural growth and then brush back into shape.

Female

1 A really even foundation is the basis of this make-up. Unless a day foundation is quite covering in texture, this is best achieved with professional bases. The ranges designed for television are excellent on stage – choose cream or water-based types. Apply with a sponge, following the manufacturer's instructions.

2 Hide tired shadows or any skin problems with a very pale concealer or cream stick foundation. Use a fine brush for precision.

3 Powder the whole face, including eyelids, with translucent, loose face powder, applying it with a velour puff or cotton wool pad rather than a brush and pressing firmly into the foundation to set it. Powder keeps shine at bay.

4 Shade the bone structure using a mid-brown powder shadow, brushing it under the cheekbones, across the tip of the nose and over the bone under the eyebrows. The shading should be subtle and carefully blended. Cheek shading is not necessary for thin faces.

5 Add colour to the cheeks using a blusher. Choose a fresh colour avoiding plum or brown tones and take it along the cheekbone, starting at the ear and finishing about halfway across the face. Brush a little over the shader under the cheekbones as well.

6 Eyes can look natural or definitely made-up according to character. A neutral tone is best, soft grey-green for white skins, lilac for darker skins. To appear natural, use highlighter over the eyelids and powder over it.

7 Line the eyes with dark brown or black according to skin and hair type. On white skins black can often make the eyes look smaller. Draw fine lines along the top and bottom eyelashes to extend them, with the top lines slightly longer than the lower ones. There should be a

Made-up look

Unmade-up look

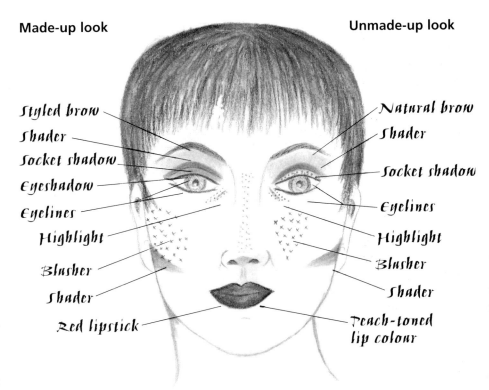

Styled brow
Shader
Socket shadow
Eyeshadow
Eyelines
Highlight
Blusher
Shader
Red lipstick

Natural brow
Shader
Socket shadow
Eyelines
Highlight
Blusher
Shader
Peach-toned lip colour

gap between these lines to open up the outer corner of the eye.

8 Brush dark brown eyeshadow along the edge of the eye socket at the top of the eyelid to give more definition to the eye. Mascara lashes.

9 Paint the mouth with lip colour suitable for the character and period. Use a lip brush for a perfect shape, working from the corners to the centre mouth on both top and bottom lips. Lining the lips before using the lipstick can be helpful. Choose a liner to match the lipstick. Plum and brown tones should be avoided as they give a dull, flat look on stage.

Black skinned actors should match their foundations to their own skin tone and choose deeper shaders, blushers and lip colours. Highlighters need to be yellow tones. Translucent powder sets all foundation shades however light or dark.

THE EYES

As the eyes reflect the thoughts of a character it is important that they can be clearly seen on stage. However, eye make-up should always be careful rather than exaggerated.

Men and boys

Eyeshadow is no longer used for male characters in normal circumstances. In small theatres all that is required is a dark brown or black line drawn along under the eyes. This shouldn't be thick or go up to the eye corners. In larger theatres add to the eye size by using a pale highlight colour on the eyelids. This will attract the light and give the effect of large eyes. Mascara is only necessary for very fair eyelashes.

Women and girls

Women need a neutral eyeshadow tone. Brown, which is popular in day make-up, actually recedes the eyes on stage. For white skins a pale grey-green and for darker skins lilac will give a neutral effect. Powder shadows are easy to apply but can be rubbed off by accident. Professional lining colours are longer lasting. Period productions will need research into the appropriate colour. Young girls' eyes should look unmade-up so highlight is used as eyeshadow. Women's eyes should have fine top and bottom eyelines and a socket shadow above the eyelids on the bone edge. Young girls only need a bottom eyeline and mascara on both top and bottom lashes. False eyelashes are applied after the whole eye make-up is finished.

Eyebrows brushed through and possibly added to
Cream highlight
Eyeline

Male eye

Shading
Socket shadow
Eyeshadow
Top eyeline
Line extension
Bottom eyeline

Female eye

Natural browshape
Shading
Socket shadow
Highlight as eyeshadow
Under-eyeline

Unmade-up female eye

THE EYEBROWS

The eyebrows frame the eyes and can also change the character of the face dramatically.

For male brows, either colour with a little cake mascara or add more definition with a well sharpened eyebrow pencil. A convincing look is achieved by drawing little hairs among the real ones. For a bushy effect, work spirit gum quickly through the brows. This is best done working against the natural growth.

Female brows need definition and if thin they disappear on stage unless clearly defined. Eyebrow shapes have changed through the centuries in fashion and during the last 100 years they have changed every decade. Carry out research to find the appropriate style for period productions.

Blocking out

Occasionally a character will need completely different eyebrows. This means blocking out the real shape. Eyebrow plastic can be rubbed through the hairs to flatten them against the skin, then make-up is used to cover the plastic and the new shape drawn over the top.

Brown-red lining colour stippled over the eyelids and drawn along the roots of the lower lashes gives an older or tired look to the eyes.

Eyebrows and lashes can be aged by brushing a small amount of highlight through them.

THE MOUTH

The two key areas of communication for an actor are the eyes and the mouth.

The shape, size and set of the mouth suggest both the temperament and mood of a character. For women the colour can suggest fashion, period and social class.

It is, however, very important that what is done to the mouth does not detract from the eyes. Whereas women can use colour, a male mouth should never be lipsticked unless there is something unusual about the character. Children should also have natural looking lips. Today a suitable lip colour for women is easily found at any cosmetic counter. As mentioned in the straight make-up section, avoid lipsticks with distinct brown or plum tones.

For period productions, certain colours are typical of different eras. The Restoration and the 1920s need bright red tones, the Victorians an unmade-up look, the 1940s need a rich blue-red and the 1960s have peach shades.

Lipstick is always better applied with a lip brush to clean, dry lips. To achieve a new shape or create an unusual one, a lip pencil can be useful.

Changing the shape

1 To make the mouth appear larger, take the lip colour over the natural outline, stopping when you reach the downy areas. Then powder the lip edge and paint a fine line of highlight around the new shape. All mouths have a natural highlight around them and this will make the mouth shape look more realistic.

2 It is more difficult to make large mouths smaller because it is easy to throw off the balance of the mouth area and give a deformed effect. Take the foundation colour well over the lip edge and then powder it. With the lip brush paint a new shape slightly within the real one. This will be more successful if a darker colour is used, which of course creates something of a problem for men. For them a shade that matches the natural lip is best.

3 Sexy lips are created by using a mid-tone lipstick and then shading the sides of the mouth with a dark colour. This gives emphasis to the centre mouth and looks provocative.

4 To twist the mouth, take foundation over the edge of one side, powder and then redraw the shape within the natural one. On the other side overdraw the shape of the top lip. A small piece of sponge placed between the lips and gums behind the overdrawn top lip will add to the effect.

5 Simple mouth ageing is easy to do by blending a little highlight over the lips. This shows up the natural lines and fades the mouth colour.

6 Teeth can be discoloured with Tooth Enamel Nicotine or a little brown shader rubbed over them. Black Tooth Enamel will block teeth out or give the effect of chipped teeth. The teeth must be dry before doing any of these things.

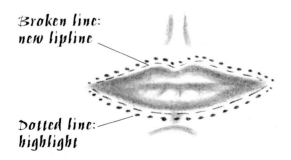

Broken line: new lipline

Dotted line: highlight

Enlarged mouth

Dotted line: highlight

Broken line: new lipline

Crooked mouth

THE NOSE

The nose is the largest feature of the face and can be used to change the look of an actor for a character. Because of its size it is easy to make mistakes, so it is always better to do too little than too much.

1 Shorten or improve the end of the nose by taking a curved shadow across the tip from nostril to nostril. The shading curves upwards.

2 Slim the nose with a highlight down the centre but not over the end.

3 Create a fat nose by highlighting the end of it and enlarging the top of the nostrils with black pencil.

4 Mortician's Wax, called commercially Naturoplast or Special Plastic, is used for building new nose shapes. It is easier to apply than the old nose putty. Glue a tiny piece of cotton wool to the skin under the wax to help to secure it and paint a layer of latex over the finished shape.

5 Warts are made by colouring a Rice Krispie or similar piece of rice breakfast cereal with brown liner and glueing it to the nose with spirit gum or eyelash adhesive.

Changing nostril shape

THE BODY AND HANDS

If a lot of body skin is showing then it will need make-up too. For normal skin tones cake make-up is used. For tanned skin, liquid body make-up gives a better effect: Kryolan do a useful colour called Carmen. A product called Fixier Spray will make it water and rub proof.

Hands need ageing for an old character:

1 Cover the hand with cake make-up – this will show up the natural lines.

2 Flatten hand and shade the hollows between the tendons. Then clench it and highlight the knuckles and bones of the fingers. Do the same with the tendons. Highlight down the centre fingers and powder.

3 With a brown pencil draw in some of the lines across the knuckles of the fingers.

4 Drop hand to expose veins and colour with blue pencil. Add liver spots with brown pencil.

The hand under stage lighting

THE FACE: BROADENING AND NARROWING

It is important to experiment with shadow and highlight so that the contours of the face can be brought out and the basic shape can appear to alter. Below are two illustrations showing the main points for broadening and narrowing the face.

Key

Highlight

Blusher

Shading

Method of broadening the face   *Method of narrowing the face*

CREATING CHARACTER

In suggesting a character through make-up, we attempt to reflect the basic nature and usual appearance of them.

Some characters are easily established: Falstaff is jovial and fat, Dracula is pale and elegant, Titania is ethereal and beautiful. With less obvious characters a little thought and research is required. The photograph here shows the character Louise from the modern Restoration play *The Art of Success* by Nick Dear. Louise gradually degenerates from the pox as the play progresses.

This is the make-up just before the play ends:

1 A grey-green foundation called Blithe Spirit 1742 is applied to give a sickly skin colour.

2 Cheekbones and eyes are hollowed with grey-brown shader and white highlights used to emphasise gauntness.

3 EF9 brown-red lining colour is blended over the eye socket area.

4 Face is powdered.

5 Scabs are made by glueing torn pieces of facial tissue to the face which are then coloured with dark-red lining colour. The area around the scabs is softly reddened.

6 Areas of green powder shadow are added for decay.

7 The hair is backcombed to give an untidy effect and then dulled with powder.

Make-up chart key

Base – Blithe Spirit
Shading – Dark grey
Highlight – White
Powder – Translucent
Eyelines/Brows – Dark brown
Decayed areas – Facial tissues coloured with EF9 and a little mid-green lining colour
Blood – Washable blood

Blended EF9

Scabs: tissue glued on and coloured with EF9 Supracolor

Shading

Black eyelines

White highlight

Base: 1742 Aquacolor

Shading: grey-brown

Mouth: natural lip colour

Blood

Green powder shadow to indicate decay

Hollowed eye: grey brown liner with added EF9

AGEING

Ageing a face effectively is difficult and requires skill as well as practice. It is all too easy to overdo the make-up so always err on the side of understatement.

Lines must be finely drawn and fit the contours of the face. Fade them carefully with a fingertip for reality. Highlights work with the lines to give the illusion of folds and looseness. They should always be wider than the lines they serve, not too close to them and well blended to avoid a striped effect. Once the foundation is applied the actor should drop their chin and look directly at themselves in the mirror. Even on quite a young person the age shadows will then appear around the eyes, nose and mouth. Trace them in carefully and blend. Screwing up the face to find lines is unwise and gives a false effect.

Age sequence

1 Unless the production requires deeper skin tones, choose a foundation two shades lighter than normal. This helps to give a loose effect to the skin. Apply thinly.

2 With a dark brown cream liner, shade in the hollows beneath the cheekbones, the temple, tired shadows under the eyes and the little dip under the nose.

3 Using a very pale cream foundation highlight the brow bones, cheekbones, centre nose, the area between tired shadows and the eyes, eyelids and the sides of the jaw beneath the ears.

4 Powder with translucent face powder avoiding smearing the highlights and shadows together.

5 Trace in age lines with dark brown pencil. These will be under the eyes, along the smile folds and at the corners of the mouth. Blend to soften.

6 Using a brush apply strokes of highlight on the inside of tired shadows and between any lines drawn there, on the outside of smile lines, on the little ridges under the nose and the fatness of the chin. Place highlights on the inside of temple shadows (see narrow face diagram). Press the end of the eyebrow inwards and highlight the fold that appears.

7 Re-powder taking care not to rub highlights and lines together.

8 Stipple a little brown-red liner on the cheekbones to break up the youthful appearance of the skin. For ruddier or rougher characters do this also on the bridge of the nose and chin.

9 Fade the lip colour with a little highlight, – this will show up the natural lines. For a stronger effect deepen the lines with brown pencil or the brown-red liner.

10 Brush through the eyebrows, working inwards to give a sparse effect; you may need to hold them in place with a little spirit gum. Then, using a fingertip, colour the brows with a little highlight to grey them. For very old characters you can highlight eyelashes too.

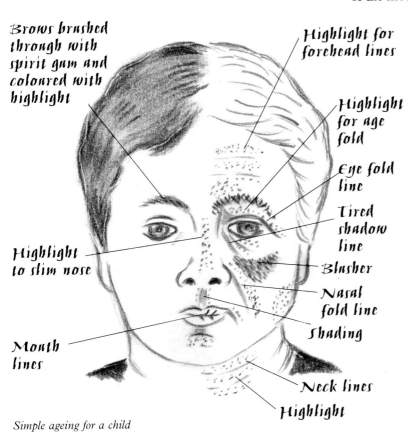

Brows brushed through with spirit gum and coloured with highlight

Highlight for forehead lines

Highlight for age fold

Eye fold line

Tired shadow line

Blusher

Nasal fold line

Shading

Highlight to slim nose

Mouth lines

Neck lines

Highlight

Simple ageing for a child

How much age?

Middle age characters may not require all these details. Also some faces appear naturally older than others and this must be taken into consideration. Children are particularly difficult to age realistically and a few well placed details are always better than attempting too much (see diagram on page 253).

Necks

Serious ageing requires the neck to be made up too. Trace broken lines along the natural ones and then add broad bands of highlight on each side of every line. Powder. Generally two lines or perhaps three at the most will be sufficient.

The forehead

Many age make-ups are ruined by crude forehead lines. An easy way to create realistic lines is this – the actor must lift their eyebrows as high as they can and whilst lifted highlight is blended across the fatness of the folds. When the eyebrows are relaxed lines will appear. If they don't, trace a couple of broken lines across the forehead where they should be.

Final thoughts

Not all old people are thin. Plumper characters will not need the shading under the cheekbones. Worried or angry characters need frown lines between the tops of the eyebrows. It is necessary to frown to find these lines, then trace one set in, ensuring that the bottom ends curve into the eyebrows. Highlight on each side of the lines. Mean and depressed characters will have slightly longer lines at the mouth corners with highlights on the outsides of them.

Colours for ageing

White skins – Male

Foundation – Cake make-up 6W or 5W
Shading – Dark brown cream liner/Supracolor
Highlights – 1W or EF85 Supracolor or Paintstick
Lines – Dark brown pencil
Powder – Translucent loose TL3
Broken veins – EF9 Supracolor

White skins – Female

Foundation – 3W Aquacolor or cream make-up
Shading – Dark brown cream liner/Supracolor
Highlights – 1W or EF85 Supracolor or Paintstick
Lines – Dark brown pencil
Powder – Translucent loose TL3
Rouge – 075
Broken veins – EF9 Supracolor

Old age mouth

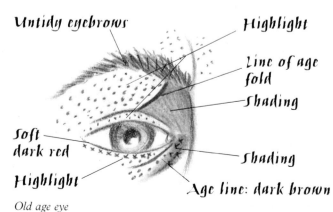

Old age eye

Black/darker skins

Foundation – to match natural skin tone

Shading – Dark brown or brown/black liner

Highlights – GG Supracolor or Paintstick

Very dark skins – Chinese Paintstick

Lines – Brown/black pencil or black depending on skin colour

Powder – Translucent loose TL3

ETHNIC FACES

In the past very stylised make-up was used for racial types but this is considered offensive in today's theatre. It is problematic, for example, for a white actor to play Othello and the best way to approach this for productions is through skin tones and definition of eyebrows and eyes. There are a number of ethnic foundations in the Kryolan range which cover most purposes. Photographs and paintings are a useful source of information for national characteristics.

Below is a diagram for an Oriental make-up. There is a lot of confusion about Oriental eye shapes – the corners do not slant up, they slant downwards. However, in Chinese and Japanese classical theatre the actors paint their eye shapes upwards. Avoid traditional 'oriental' foundation colours like Chinese, Oriental and yellow. Most Orientals do not have yellow skin tones and a flatter look of the face can be achieved with a lighter foundation.

Oriental eye make-up

HAIR

Always be ready to change the style and possibly the colour of the hair for a character. Nowadays there are excellent spray-on colours available from theatrical stockists and all chemists stock semi-permanent rinses which wash out with a few shampoos.

Greying hair

A silver spray is the best way of tackling this as it gives a realistic sheen to the hair. Hair powder or talc will give a very dead look and is not advisable. To grey small areas like the sides of the face, moustaches and beards, use a very pale panstik type of make-up. Apply with fingertips and lightly stroke the colour over the surface of the hair. A toothbrush is not a good idea here as it tends to make people use too much make-up.

Wigs

Obviously it is better and cheaper to use the actor's own hair whenever possible but this is not always feasible. This is where wigs come in but they can be expensive to hire and require careful handling. Basically two types are available – hair lace wigs (real hair or synthetic fibres knotted on to a hair lace cap), and synthetic stretch wigs. Hair lace wigs have fine hairlines and are generally used when the style is dressed back off the face. Stretch wigs have a heavier front hairline which looks very noticeable if the hair is dressed back. Theatrical wig stockists supply both types.

When budgets are tight, cheap synthetic wigs from high street stores and fashion wig stockists can be an excellent alternative. The most versatile style in this type is mid-length and softly curled. It can be dressed into most styles, backcombed smooth and takes coloured sprays well. These wigs can be styled dry or wet and set with rollers.

Keeping the actor's own hair in place

Unless the hair is quite short it will need to be secured in some way to prevent it from slipping out from under the wig. The best and cheapest way of preventing this is

A stocking cap used to secure hair

with a stocking cap which fits tightly over the head holding the hair in place. You use the top end of the stocking, not the foot, and the correct sort is a high denier non stay-up type. Tights will not do. Place the stocking over the hair and cut, leaving sufficient to make a small knot on the top of the head.

Putting wigs on

Always apply make-up before the wig. It is advisable to have help in putting on a wig – four hands are generally better than two.

Hair lace wigs

The actor should hold the hair lace front and together with a helper carefully pull the wig over the head, firstly positioning it well down the forehead. Once it is over the hair, move it back to the correct position on the forehead. Then the hair lace will need to be glued down with spirit gum. To do this properly the lace needs to be pulled taut across the forehead and down in front of the ears. When it is as taut as possible place a good dab of matt spirit gum under each of the lace flaps in front of the ears and hold in position until completely dry. Matt spirit gum is best for this as it does not catch the light. The lace should now 'disappear' when viewed from the audience. If the front edge is frilly, place dots of gum at intervals along under the edge and press the net firmly to the skin with a velour puff or soft, dry sponge.

Never apply make-up to the hair lace if you can avoid it as it will show up the edge of the lace.

Crossed kirby grips

Making a pincurl

Synthetic wigs

Unless it has been elaborately dressed, it is easier to put on this type of wig by placing your hands inside it, stretching it slightly as you pull it on to your head. If it is elaborately dressed, follow the advice for the hair lace wig to put it on. Stretch wigs have a habit of lifting up at the back of the head so that it is advisable to attach them to the stocking cap with Kirby grips at the nape of the neck. It is also wise to put two grips just above the ears to secure the wig there as well, but be careful to ensure that they don't show – Kirby grips pick up easily under stage lighting.

Hair length problems

Two lengths in particular are problematic for wigs – very short and very long hair. The problem with very short hair is that the wig slips around on it and a stocking top is no help. The professional solution is wig springs. These tiny springs catch on to the hair and then pins can be pushed through the wig and under them, thus securing it. Care has to be taken when removing them. Long hair causes problems because it is difficult to put up under a wig without falling down or distorting the head shape. One solution is to put the hair into pincurls all over the head – this works best with shoulder length hair.

The other way, which is ideal for really long hair, is wrapping. This is how to do it:

1 Part the hair down the centre of the head from the forehead to the nape of the neck, then pincurl one side out of the way.

2 Brush the other side across the back of the head as smoothly as possible and secure with Kirby grips.

3 Bring the rest of the hair over across this and secure with grips.

4 Tidy the ends, pin them flat and spray the head with hairspray. Then carefully stretch a stocking top over the hair and tuck in any stray bits.

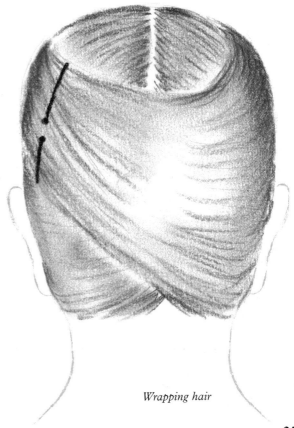

Wrapping hair

257

MAKING BEARDS AND MOUSTACHES

Ready-made facial hairpieces are mounted on hair lace in the same way as lace-edged wigs. However it is relatively easy to make the simpler shapes from crêpe hair. Crêpe hair is available in a limited range of natural colours and also primary colours like yellow and red. Sometimes you will need to mix two shades together for the right effect. The hair can be applied directly to the skin or on to a base of two layers of liquid latex. Always trace the shape that you hope to achieve on to the face before you begin.

Preparing crêpe hair

Crêpe hair is supplied in plaits knotted on to two lengths of string. For most purposes the hair will need to be straightened before applying to the face. There are two ways of doing this.

Steaming

Loosen the crêpe hair from the string and cut off a good length. Hold it with both hands and carefully stretch it taut over a steaming kettle spout, moving it gradually to straighten the amount that you need. Dry on a towel.

Ironing

This is the safe way. Place the length of hair on to an ironing board and cover with a damp cloth. Press. If you have a steam iron, all that you need to do is put the iron over one end and gently pull the hair along under the plate, flattening it.

1 *Fairly thick hairs arranged vertically.*

2 *Thicker version of 1. Ends fall to sides of mouth – the 'walrus' type, typical of 1914-18 period.*

3 *Hairs arranged horizontally with a slight upward sweep.*

4 *Another horizontal arrangement with the tips waxed or gummed military style.*

5 *Hairs arranged vertically under the nose and gradually spread more horizontally towards the cheeks. Vertical hairs under the lower lip.*

6 *As 5, but with hairs lengthened to the chin and below – typical of the 17th century (Charles I).*

Applying the crêpe hair

Moustaches can be made on a latex base. Before beginning draw your shape and paint on two layers of theatrical liquid latex, drying the skin between them. Then glue the crêpe hair on to this base. When the moustache is removed, the back of the latex will require powdering to prevent it curling and sticking to itself.

Only the very thinnest of moustaches, the David Niven types, should be made with one layer of hair. You will generally require at least two. To achieve Diagram 1 you will need two layers, Diagram 2, three layers and Diagram 3, two or three worked sideways. For Diagram 4 you will need two narrow layers, again worked sideways, Diagram 5, two layers for the moustache and one for the lip beard and Diagram 6, two layers with three for the goatee.

Position of layers

Angle hair to suit shape

(3)
(2)
(1)

Begin at lip edge

Laying a crêpe hair moustache

A good effect succeeds or fails on the way that the hair is handled. Always use a fairly long piece or you will have difficulty in holding it. Feather the layer of hair out so that it will all attach to the glue and angle it to suit the moustache shape. As you build up the layers, press them well into the glue with a brush handle or soft, dry sponge. Trim carefully when the whole shape is finished.

Beards are more difficult to achieve well. Again bear in mind the angle of the hair and follow these instructions:

1 Start under the chin and work outwards along the jawline.

2 Place a second piece on the front of the chin under the lower lip and take to the sides above the previous application. (It would be necessary to trim both stages 1 and 2 if the beard were required for the chin only.)

3 For a full beard, continue from 2, applying more hair under the lower lip and thickening the 'sideboards' running up the sides of the face.

4 If a moustache is required in addition, follow suggestions on the opposite page and blend in with the beard.

5 Blend into face make-up with a few brown or black hairlike strokes of colour or a grey liner in order to graduate the hair tones into the skin.

Applying a ready-made facial hairpiece

With moustaches in particular it is wise to apply a layer of spirit gum to the area and let it dry prior to actually glueing the piece on. This prevents sweat from coming through and dislodging the facial hair. If available, use medicated spirit gum, particularly for young sensitive skins. Then apply another layer of glue and press the piece on, centring it first of all and then working along to the sides. Press the net edge firmly into the skin with a dry sponge or cloth. Side whiskers should be pressed up as close to the real hair as possible to avoid a telltale gap.

Stage 1– fix hair under chin

Stage 2 – add to front of chin and jaw line

Stage 3 – jaw, to lower lip and moustache if required

FANTASY CHARACTERS

These characters can be enjoyable to create but require discipline, otherwise the fun of doing them can spoil the end result. It is wise to design the look on paper to begin with, keeping it as simple as possible – the busier the design the less effective it will be. There is a wonderful range of unusual shades available in theatrical make-up stockists ranging from gold and silver through to bright primary colours. For a white face choose T.V. clown-white Aquacolor which gives an excellent finish. White is possibly the most difficult colour to apply evenly and requires patience. A useful colour to be aware of is 1742 Blithe Spirit, a pale grey green. Used thinly it is marvellous for scary characters like ghosts and vampires. Used more densely it is a wonderful base for fairies, sea creatures and ethereal characters. Care needs to be taken with silver and gold as they can distort the face with their shine. Glitter is fun for some characters but again discretion is needed when using it and it works best on cheekbones and eyes. Unless the character has no relationship to a human form it is very important to allow the eyes good emphasis within a fantasy make-up.

Animals

It will be very helpful to have a front and side view of the animal in question. Make a chart defining the key elements of the creature. Most importantly, be sure to obscure the human nose shape and mouth.

Fairies

These are usually pretty characters, and pastel skin tones shaded with a darker version of the base colour and highlighted with white works well. If Aquacolors are used as foundations they can also be painted on to the hair.

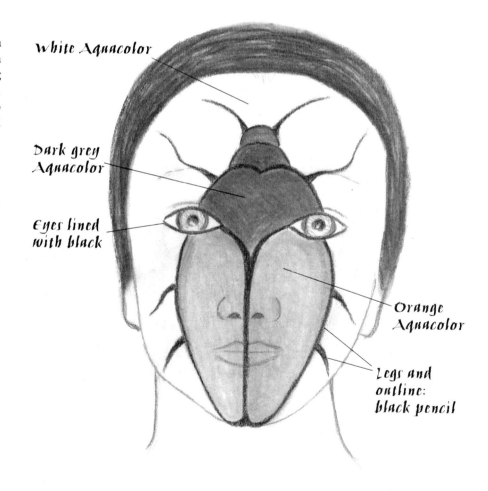

White Aquacolor

Dark grey Aquacolor

Eyes lined with black

Orange Aquacolor

Legs and outline: black pencil

The Click Beetle from The Insect Play

Ghosts

1742 Blithe Spirit is the colour for these. Shade the face either with dark grey or EF9 Supracolor which gives a particularly ghoulish effect on the grey-green base. Highlights are done with a white cream foundation like Supracolor or Paintstick. Teeth can be broken or hidden with black tooth enamel.

Space creatures

There are so many designs from film and television for creatures from other worlds that it is impossible to give a general example. However, metallic colours work well in this category of make-up as they give an effective non-human appearance. The addition of half masks, added pieces, crêpe hair and wax can all develop an interesting character. Again simplicity is the key to a good make-up.

When using strong colours, always trace the design on the face first and then colour in working from the forehead downwards to avoid smudging your work.

Foundation: silver-blue Aquacolor

Eyebrows blocked out and redrawn in higher shape with black pencil

White Aquacolor

Mid-blue eyeshadow

Dark blue socket shadow

Black eyelines

Silver glitter

Blue-green Aquacolor

Dark blue

Dark blue lip line

Mid-blue lip colour

Simple fantasy make-up based on shades of blue

ARTIFICIAL FEATURES

Scars

There are a number of ways to create scarring. The simplest way is with a creme liner called EF9 which is a dark brown-red colour. If you cannot find it, try mixing a bright red liner with a clear dark brown one. With all simple scars you will always achieve a more realistic effect if you pat an area of faded red in the basic shape on to the face before painting on the actual scar. Then, using a fine brush, paint the dark red down the centre of the faded red, being sure not to let it come too close to the ends. Set with powder.

There is a liquid called collodion, which contracts the skin and is useful for creating pulled old scars. This is most effective when used on the looser areas of the face and mustn't be used close to eyes or on sensitive skin. Remove it with surgical spirit or spirit gum remover.

Facial padding

Characters such as Falstaff or Henry VIII need to appear plumper. It always helps to begin by using a paler foundation which will fill out the face under stage lighting. For men or boys, a female foundation would be good. Women and girls will require a shade two degrees paler than normal. The simplest way to pad the face is with small pieces of sponge inserted into the mouth between the skin and the teeth. There is room for this at the sides of the top lip and tucked down behind the bottom lip. The sponge pieces need not be large as they will distort the speech. They should also be placed to the sides rather than centrally, which would look odd rather than fat.

Blood

Stage blood is sold in liquid and powder forms. You can also sometimes find a jelly version in fancy dress make-up kits which is useful for a 'wet' effect. Try to buy washable blood for obvious reasons. Blood also comes in capsules which when bitten combine with saliva and foam from the mouth. For weals and lash marks follow the advice for scars and add a little blood at intervals across them. Put it in an eye-dropper if you need drips. Stage blood dries and flakes easily so it is best to apply it just before going on stage.

Prosthetic noses

Latex and rubber noses can be used for a very big effect. It is best to apply the nose after foundation and powder and then colour to match the skin tone. Use cream or grease make-up which will preserve your false piece. If the edge is rather thick, the only solution is to paint liquid latex over it to soften the line before you colour the nose.

Perspiration

Perspiration can be simulated by mixing glycerine and water to the required consistency. Apply it from a spray bottle or with a soft sponge.

Tears

If the actor cannot produce natural tears, eye drops make a suitable substitute.

Faded EF9 liner (use finger to apply)

EF9 on brush. Shape wider in centre, narrow at ends

Simple scar using EF9 lining colour

Bald caps

Every so often a production requires a bald-headed character, which generally means that a bald cap is needed for the actor in question. Bald caps are not easy to use and if badly applied can look extremely obvious. Usually this is because the cap is ill-fitting or the person putting it on doesn't know the correct way to do it.

Here are a few tips for a well fitted result. Let's begin by looking at the types that are available. Ready-made latex caps come in small, medium and large sizes. They are generally heavy duty and the edge of the cap can be quite difficult to hide. Glatzen caps are also quite durable and come in one stretchable size. However, the best one to use is probably the Pre-impression cap (made of a thinner Glatzen material) which has a much finer front edge. The only drawback is that it can tear quite easily so must be handled with care.

Tracing a cutting line

Choosing the cap

It is wise to measure the actor's head for size and choose one that fits snugly. This will help to avoid wrinkles on the top of the head when the cap is on.

Fitting the cap

The actor's hair needs to be brushed back and tucked behind the ears before beginning. Hair spray will hold it in position. Long hair, which can give a deformed appearance under a cap, will need to be carefully wrapped around the head and held in place with tape (hairpins and grips cannot be used under a cap as they will split it). It is extremely difficult for an actor to fit a cap successfully by themselves. Someone is needed to stretch it over the hair and to do the back.

Once the cap is on, a cutting line needs to be traced allowing for forehead wrinkles and a snug fit around the ears. Always spirit gum the forehead edge first and then stretch the cap down in front of the ears and glue there. When this is quite dry the actor should drop their head so that the back of the cap can be stretched tightly down the neck and securely glued in place.

Trim away any excess cap and colour it with bald cap grease or Paintstick and powder the surface.

The finished look

MASKS – 1:
Papier mâché method

Masks have always played an important part in the theatre. Primitive man used to wear a mask for hunting, disguising himself as the animal he was stalking.

Egyptian priests used animal head masks to represent gods. Roman tragic actors wore large head masks – some of terrifying aspect according to contemporary reports.

The medieval mystery plays also made use of masks to portray devils; actors portraying buffoons also wore masks.

Masks of various shapes and kinds were frequently worn for masked balls (as in 'Romeo and Juliet') and are today enjoying a revival in the form of the carnival heads used by travelling players in America (Bread and Puppet Theatre and other groups).

Clay model method of construction

One of the most practical methods of making masks is on a clay model mould. The illustrations here show the materials and process of making a full-face mask:

1 You will need a smooth, flat board, sufficient clay for the size of head (Plasticine can be used if available), Vaseline or any thick oil, newspaper and tissue paper, cold-water paste and brush, string and elastic for tying, and paint.

'worm' of clay to build up eyebrow

2 Using the board as a base, model the shape you require. Work coils and lumps of clay to make bold vigorous shapes – avoid undercutting which would allow the mask to stick to the clay.

When modelling is complete, allow the clay to dry then grease the surface thoroughly. Alternatively, if time is short, build up tissue on the moist clay immediately.

3 Cover the greased surface with a single layer of torn, unpasted tissue paper. A damped brush is ideal for picking up the small pieces of tissue. When the clay has been covered, paste the whole surface. This first layer acts as a smooth barrier between the clay model and newspaper.

Start building up the paper layers – six are sufficient – with torn squares of newspaper (about 25 mm square).

To ensure even distribution, alternate layers of white and coloured newspaper (colour with dye or ink by soaking pieces in a bowl). A layer of butter muslin on the fifth layer will help to strengthen the mask.

gently lift mask from mould

mould

4 Prise the mask from the clay model when the paper is quite dry. Take care not to damage the clay if a repeat is required.

turning edges over and pasting down

PASTE

5 Mould papier-mâché round all the edges, pasting down loose bits of paper inside. Cut out eye-holes and paste the edges smooth. Leave the mask to dry thoroughly.

holes for elastic

6 Smooth the mask with fine sandpaper and apply shellac all over. The shellac will bind together any loose pieces and prepare the surface for painting. Pierce holes at temple position to carry elastic.

string or wool hair

holes for eyes cut out
painted surface

elastic attached here

7 Paint mask to suit the character desired. Add hair with string, coarse wool or other materials – colour the hair to match the face before glueing. Attach elastic.

Wire mask

A stronger mask can be built on a wire frame as illustrated below:

wire frame

tapes between wire

50x50mm papier mâché

Build a wire contour to the shape required. Strengthen between the wires with self-adhesive masking tape.

Apply five or six layers of newspaper pieces (as described on the opposite page) and complete as before.

Add hair and other features with string, felt or other materials.

MASKS – 2

Sometimes half-face or eye masks are required rather than the full-face masks.

Eye masks

elastic as an alternative to stick support

shellaced felt or papier mâché

sequins or other ornaments may be glued to mask

painted lines

thin dowel glued and taped to side of mask – paint to match

Small eye masks do not require a model or mould, but felt can be shaped to the face by stiffening with shellac for self-supporting types (see illustration) or can be fitted with elastic and not stiffened for wearing on the head.

Half-face masks

These masks allow freedom to speak. Make-up must be adjusted to suit the colouring of the mask.

hair brushed over top edge of mask

mask built over clay mould

Half-face masks need more modelling. Make a clay or Plasticine model on a board and build up in papier-mâché as described on the previous two pages.

266

Carnival masks

Very large heads, used mainly for carnivals but occasionally in the theatre (see page 268) can be built over a wire-mesh framework.

Cut a piece of wire-mesh approximately 1 m × 1.30 m and shape into a cylinder; overlap and bend over the edges and thread through with string or wire to fasten. Make up individual features with added pieces of wire-mesh, joining and fastening with additional wire.

flap down

Cut slits in the cylinder from the top and bottom edges and shape with mesh over the top of the head, overlapping as necessary – also draw in the mesh round the neck area over an upturned bucket. Tie together all overlapping areas and flatten out all points.

separate mesh pieces for each feature

bucket for stability whilst constructing

Cover the whole head with 5 or 6 layers of newspaper in 20 cm squares, using cold-water paste. Allow to dry thoroughly.

Secure foam rubber or plastic inside the neck to avoid scratching. Cut suitable eye-holes and cover with gauze or muslin. Add two pairs of tapes to the base of the neck, front and back, long enough to secure the head around the waist of the actor.

Paint to suit the character, adding materials for hair, etc. if required. Avoid painting the eye gauzes with thick colour.

gauze eye-holes
foam rubber protection
tapes for securing to armpits or waist

Animal masks

stitch ears here

fold and stitch ears to head

stitch mane to central piece

5 mm. cuts in mane

make up face to match mask

These masks can be made by the methods already described, or with foam rubber.

The donkey mask above shows a method that can be used and adapted to suit most animals. The advantage of foam rubber is the ease with which masks can be made and decorated. Foam rubber takes colour extremely well – all features can be added with fibre and felt-tip pens.

The cutting pattern given above is intended only as a guide to structure. Design and make shapes by experimenting.

Above: papier mâché masks taken from clay models before smoothing and painting (see also 264).

Decorative masks

Should a purely decorative mask be required for fixing on a wall or large flat area, use expanded polystyrene. It is easy to cut this material with hot wires (page 147) and build it up in light relief. It can then be painted – see example below. A useful thickness to work with is 25 mm. Pieces can be glued on with P.V.A. medium or polystyrene adhesive.

See overleaf for more examples of masks

267

Examples of masks

Left: carnival masks.
A group of young children in masks made by 12 year old boys. In rehearsal for a carnival procession which opened a school production of 'Twelfth Night' (see page 266).

Below: animal masks. A scene from 'Noah' by André Obey. Masks are of canvas but similar ones could be built up from foam plastic.

Glossary

STAGE TERMS · LISTS OF MATERIALS
SUPPLIERS · INDEX

GLOSSARY

Technical terms related to the stage

Apron The forestage extending into the auditorium beyond the proscenium arch. Usually at stage level but sometimes built lower. (see page 5)

Arena An acting area surrounded by the audience, either totally or on three (sometimes two) sides. (see pages 5 and 6)

Backcloth Sometimes called a backdrop. A scene canvas across the width of the upstage, fixed at the top and bottom. (see page 23)

Backing Any flat or cloth behind doors or windows to mask parts of the stage that should not be seen. (see model stage on page 77)

Bar or **Barrel** An iron pipe above the stage for carrying lighting equipment and scenery. Fastened in a vertical position, it is called a boom. (see page 180)

Batten 1 Electrical: the compartment trough carrying a set of lamps divided into 3 or 4 circuits. (see page 176)

2 Scenic: lengths of timber for tautening backcloths at top and bottom. The top edge of a cloth is gripped between two battens, termed sandwich battens. A batten is often slotted through a canvas hem.

Book flats Two flats hinged together to fold to any angle. (see page 51)

Boom See **Bar**.

Border Horizontal flat or curtain, hanging from bar or grid to mask lights and/or ceiling from the audience. (see diagram and page 18)

Box set An enclosed setting that has three walls and usually a ceiling. (see page 88)

Brace An extending rod with attachments to support flats (see page 55). A **French Brace** is hinged. (see page 55)

Brail The rope and adjusting part of hanging scenery. (see diagram)

Centre line A line from front to back of stage on the ground plan drawing – chalked on the stage itself for correct placing of settings and props. (see page 79)

Cleat Metal fitting on the back of flats to which a throw-line is attached. (see page 54)

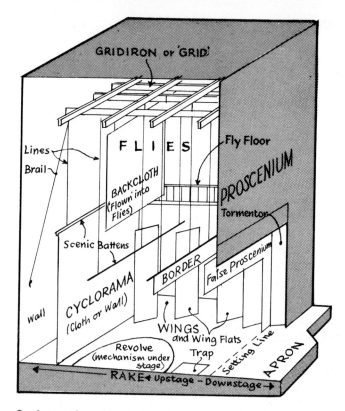

Section cut through centre line showing parts of traditional theatre stage. All terms included on the drawing are explained in the glossary.

Cloth see **Backcloth**.

Cut-out A cloth with parts cut away to suggest foliage etc. (see pages 24 and 58)

Cut-out flat A flat with a plywood or hardboard edge cut away to suggest foliage, etc. (see page 51)

Cyclorama Either a permanent plaster wall or, more frequently, a curved or straight backcloth hung at the rear of the stage. Used as sky or background, usually painted white and lit as required. (see pp. 26 and 92)

Dimmer (correct electrical term: a **rheostat**) An electrical appliance which varies intensity of light. (see page 179)

Dip Metal trap in the stage floor for electrical sockets – used for plugging in stage floor lights. (see page 181)

Dock Backstage storage area for scenery.

Downstage Towards the audience.

Elevation Side view drawings of units or parts shown on the ground plan. (see page 80)

False proscenium A smaller temporary 'proscenium' of flats or cloths behind the main proscenium arch to make the stage area smaller:

Flat A rectangular wooden frame covered with canvas, hardboard or other material. The unit of which most scenery is composed. (see pages 47–70)

Flies The space above the stage where sets can be 'flown' or taken up (not usually provided in school theatres).

Floats see **Footlights**.

Flood Lamp giving a wide spread of light. (see page 175)

Fly floor Galleries above stage on side walls used for securing, raising and lowering lights and scenery – only found over large, traditional stages. (see illustration on this page)

F.O.H. see **Front of House**

Footlights An electrical batten at the front of the stage at floor level. (see page 180)

Fresnel A spotlight with a soft-edge lens. (see page 177)

Front cloth A movable cloth immediately behind the proscenium arch (see page 18)

Front of House Term sometimes applied to the auditorium area, usually abbreviated to F.O.H.

Front of House lighting Spotlights positioned in or above the auditorium area to illumine the forestage. (see pages 181 and 182)

Frost A gelatine ('gel') lighting filter that resembles frosted glass – for diffusing light. (see page 186)

Gauze A transparent cloth for scenic effects – called also a transparency. (see pages 24–25)

Gelatine ('gel') A colour filter for lighting. (see page 186)

Grid Wooden or steel framework above large stages for suspending all equipment, scenery and lighting; used for storage between scenes. (see illustration on this page)

Ground plan A scaled drawing of a setting seen from above. (see page 79)

Ground row **1** Electrical: batten lighting for a cyclorama at stage floor level. (see page 181)

2 Scenic: a flat lying on its side across the stage concealing lighting, and giving impression of ramparts, undulating ground, etc. according to the shape of its cut-out top edge. (see page 58)

Hang iron Ring on iron plate secured to the back of flats – used on stages where scenery can be flown. (see **Flies**) (see page 56)

House curtain The proscenium curtains, also called 'front tabs' or 'house tabs'. (see page 18)

House lights Lights in the auditorium: the normal hall lights, not to be confused with lights placed F.O.H. for stage lighting purposes.

Inset A small scene within a larger setting. (see page 106)

Legs Canvas wings, hanging vertically as side maskings. (see page 116)

Lines Hemp ropes used for raising and lowering scenery and lights. They are fastened to cleats on the sides of the stage, on the fly galleries – or to a grid when scenery and battens are held in permanent place. The lines run through a series of pulleys:

Lines and pulleys suspended from grid.

Glossary (continued)

Mask   To hide parts of the stage from the audience.

Opposite prompt (Stage Right)   The right-hand side of the stage when facing the audience (the opposite side from the prompter in Britain) – abbreviated to O.P. (see stage plan on this page)

Plate   A reinforcing corner, usually of plywood, for strengthening the frames of flats at butt corners. (see page 49)

Pre-set (pre-setting) **1** In large lighting control systems, the capacity to set up in advance any lighting arrangement. By pressing different master switches one scenic effect will be cross-faded for another.

2 The lighting seen on stage before the play begins.

Priming   Coat of thin size and paint as a preparation for painting. (see page 113)

Profile spot   Hard-edge spotlight, also called a 'mirror spot'. (see page 177)

Prompt side (Stage Left)   The left-hand side of the stage when facing the audience (the side where the prompter usually sits in Britain) – abbreviated to P.S. (see stage plan on this page)

Properties (**'props'**)   All objects on stage too small to be classified as scenery – they include all furniture. (see pages 133–172)

Proscenium   The stage opening that separates the audience from the actors on the traditional type of stage.

Rail   Horizontal part of the framework of a flat. (see page 48)

Rake   The slope of the stage floor from the back down to the front on some larger stages. (see illustration on previous page of glossary)

Return   A flat leading off at right angles to another. (see page 57)

Reveal   A small 'return' surrounding an arch, window or doorway to show the thickness of the wall. (see page 60)

Revolve   A revolving turntable for carrying two scenes for a quick change – only on large stages. The turntable can be permanent or temporary. (see illustration on page 270 of glossary)

Rostrum   **1** Platform for raising parts of a stage level. **2** One of a series of rostra for building an independent stage. (see pages 27–46)

Set piece   Short piece of 'ground row,' e.g. a shrub or bush. (see page 156)

Setting line   A line set back from the front edge of the stage, slightly behind the proscenium (except on an apron stage) drawn on the ground plan and chalked on the stage floor in order to position scenery and props. (see page 79)

Sight lines   The limits of stage visible to the audience – shown as lines on plans. (see pages 16–17)

Sill   Iron bar screwed to the bottom of door flats for strengthening and securing. (see page 62)

Stage cloth   A cloth laid over the stage to reduce noise, seldom used on small stages. Where used it is often painted to match the setting.

Stage left   Right of stage, looking from auditorium.

Stage right   Left of stage, looking from auditorium. (see plan)

up stage right	up stage centre	up stage left
centre stage right	centre stage	centre stage left
down stage right	down stage centre	down stage left
O.P.		P.S.

Stage screw   Screw for fixing braces to the stage floor – not recommended except for strong permanent stage floors. Alternative is a **stage weight** for holding brace in position. (see page 55)

Stile   Vertical part of the framework of a flat. (page 48)

Tabs   Curtains.

Throw-line   Line for lashing two flats together. (see page 54)

Toggle On large flats, the supports to the centre rail. (see page 48)

Tormentor A black masking flat behind the proscenium at right angles – or angled upstage. Sometimes used as a false proscenium. (see glossary illustration on page 270)
The setting line is usually drawn from the upstage edge of the tormentors.

Trap A door in the stage floor for special effects and entrances – usually in large theatres. (see glossary illustration on page 270)

Traverse tabs Tabs on a track across the stage, on a line with a set of wings and borders. (see page 18)

Truck A mobile rostrum carrying a section of the setting – resting on wheels or ball-castors. (see page 42)

Upstage Towards the back of the stage.

Wings 1 The flats masking the sides of the stage. (see glossary illustration on page 270)
2 The sides of the stage masked from view by the wings or wing flats.
3 Legs – hanging canvas wings.

COMPLETE LIST OF MATERIALS, TOOLS AND SUNDRIES
Basic materials

Wood

Softwood (pine, etc.) – see chart on page 69 for metric sizes

Plywood – assorted thicknesses and sizes

Hardboard – assorted thicknesses and sizes

Composition boards such as 'Weyroc'

Balsa wood for modelling

Bamboo and *cane* for properties

Metals

Thin sheet aluminium and alloys for properties, arms and armour.

Wire – thin gauge 1 mm
medium gauge 1.6 mm
thick gauge 2.5 mm

Wire mesh – for use in constructing set pieces of shrubs, sculpture, etc.

Foils – all colours for scenic effects, properties, etc.

Metal scrap – small pieces of chain, bottle caps, coins, sequins, glitter, fine binding wire: all ideal for decorating properties, etc.

Paper and card

Newspaper for general purposes

Grey sugar paper for papier mâché (stronger than newspaper)

Brown parcel paper – for properties

Tissue for papier mâché and details such as imitation glass

Cartridge paper for sketches and plans

Corrugated cardboard – general purpose material for scale models and properties

Cardboard – useful for leg armour and large properties

Strawboard – useful for the stiff parts of properties

Cloth

Flax canvas – for flats and backcloths

Scenery hessian – cheap form of covering for flats; also useful for properties

Bolton twill – used for curtain settings

Scenery gauze for transformation

Felt and underfelt – available in various qualities; used for properties and armour

Old blankets – armour-making

Sheeting – generally useful for properties and armour

Buckram – useful for making helmets and other headgear

Gauze bandages for small properties

Butter muslin – ideal for strengthening and supporting irregular properties: sculptures, masks, etc.

Hessian scrim – about 75 mm wide; open mesh scrim useful in combination with plaster for sculptural properties

Muslin scrim – about 50 mm wide; fine mesh scrim for sculptural details and as a reinforcement for plaster moulds

Continued overleaf

Modelling materials

Plasticine – useful general-purpose material for smaller items

Clay – ideal for mask models

Papier mâché

Fine paper pulp

Plaster – used with scrim, ideal for large properties

Expanded polystyrene – versatile plastic material for properties, textured surfaces and printing blocks

Making and shaping

Essential tools

Hand and tenon saws

Coping saw

Fretsaw

Hacksaws, large and small

Plane

Chisels – assorted sizes

Mallet

'Surform' shaping tools

Claw and tack hammers

Hand stapler

Screwdrivers – assorted

'G' clamps and cramps

Brace and bits

Hand-drill and set of twist drills

Pliers and pincers

Tin snips and wire cutters

Adjustable spanner

Files and rasps

'Stanley' trimming knife

Try-square

Mortice gauge

Dividers and a pair of large compasses

Nail punch

Bucket – assorted sizes, some at least of galvanised metal

Useful tools

An electric drill and attachments

Jig-saw

Rip-saw for large pieces of wood

Grinding wheel

Fillers

Materials for use in filling holes, shaping awkward areas, curves, etc. in small items of scenery and in properties

Alabastine, plaster of Paris – very fine, tough, white plasters

Fibre-glass – specialist material suitable for those with knowledge of its uses in boat-building, etc. Can be used as a basic structure for helmets, armour and properties

Thistle/pink plaster – cheaper, coarser plaster, useful for textural effects

Polyfilla – plastic filler, very tough and durable

Papier mâché – can be home-made or can be bought from certain craft or toy shops (expensive)

Wood filler – plastic wood. Can be useful in detailed model-making

Sawdust and glue – home-made mixture for large gaps and cracks in rough work.

Smoothing materials

Garnet paper – long-lasting and tough abrasive

Sandpaper (or glasspaper) – graded from very fine to coarse, abrasive for general purposes

Files (see *Tools*) – various

Surform tools – wide range of shaping files and planes

Fixing and fastening

Adhesives

Animal glues – traditional glues ideal for wood joints but not waterproof. Sold by weight as 'pearl' crystals, sheet or solid bars and in branded containers such as Croid Aero Glue, Duroglue, Lepage's Liquid Glue.

Size powder – for scenic painting

Casein glue – stronger wood glue than animal glue where very strong joints required – sold in powder form under the brand name Cascanite.

Contact cements – the two surfaces are glued and, when brought together, 'impact' and are difficult to move.

Bostik No. 1 is a lightweight adhesive, effective for model making settings and card props

Evo-stik Impact 528 is more powerful for stronger jobs

Epoxies – compound adhesive for very strong fixing; ideal for repairs to glass, china, etc. (slow drying). Brand names include Araldite and Twinbond.

Latex – excellent for fabrics, paper and card; very quick drying. Brand names include Copydex, Jiffytex, Kaytex

SYNTHETIC RESINS: PLASTIC RESINS

Under this general heading are some of the most versatile of adhesives: P.V.A., P.V.C. and Acrylic.

P.V.A. (Polyvinyl acetate)

The most versatile for general theatre work, ideal for strong adhesion of wood, fabric and plastic.

Thinned slightly with water, it also a useful painting medium for mixing powder colours.

Brand names include Marvin Medium and Evo-Stik W.

P.V.C. (*Polyvinyl chloride*)
Useful for flexible plastics – curtains, etc. Brand names include Plastifex and Plastisol.

Acrylic (*Polymethyl acrylate*)
A painting medium and an adhesive for fabrics, card and paper. Brand names include Alocryl and Nacryl. All synthetic resins can be thinned in water but are waterproof when dry. The solvent to use for hardened brushes is methylated spirit.

Tapes and string

Sellotape – plastic tape (clear or coloured) sticky on one side

Masking tape – similar to Sellotape but less strongly adhesive. Useful for masking areas not to be painted, etc. and removable.

Gummed paper tape – for paper and card.

Insulating tape – similar to Sellotape but more pliable. Used for covering wire – electrical or otherwise.

String and cord – picture cord, nylon, hemp, etc. all useful for binding and holding.

Rope – hemp or nylon for scenic purposes

Elastic bands – to hold materials while modelling

Cotton and synthetic thread – for sewing and fastening costumes and props

General ironmongery

Screws Countersunk steel: $1''$, $1\frac{1}{4}''$, $1\frac{1}{2}''$, $1\frac{3}{4}''$, $2''$, $2\frac{1}{2}''$ and $3''$
Round head: $\frac{1}{2}''$ and $1''$

Nails Oval: $1''$, $1\frac{1}{2}''$, $2''$ and $2\frac{1}{2}''$
Round: $1''$, $1\frac{1}{2}''$, $2''$ and $2\frac{1}{2}''$

Assorted nuts and bolts

Pins – veneer and panel (or gimp), all useful for small, detailed work

Tacks – for fastening canvas

Corrugated fasteners – useful for simple butt joints

Ball catches – quick and efficient for door fixing

Hasp and staple (*gate hook and eye*) – for large boxes, trunks or doors

Hinges – assorted collection

Brackets – assortment for supporting shelves, joining pieces of wood at a right angle, etc.

Angle (*mild steel*) – useful for supports, reveals, etc. Less strong than brackets.

Rawlplugs – for securing large scenery or equipment to the walls

Stapler and staples of various sizes

Decorating

Paint

Decorator's powder (*scenic*) – colour for scene-painting

Powder colour (*tempera*) – general-purpose colour for props

Enamel and Lacquer – for detailed props requiring high gloss

Metallic powders – powders in gold, silver, green, blue and mauve shades

Dyes – aniline dyes for fabrics. Brand names include Dylon which can be used hot or cold.

Medium, thinner and solvent

P.V.A. medium – versatile liquid base for mixing colour or metallic powders – and for glueing fabrics and papers (see *Adhesives*). Marvin Medium is one of the best-known.

Gold Size – for mixing metallic powders

Varnish – use clear varnish for a high gloss finish on some props, jewellery, etc.

Shellac (available flake or liquid) – a varnish for stiffening felt and for waterproofing and hardening props and armour (clear type for props)

Turpentine (*turps*), *white spirit*, *methylated spirit* – all essential solvents for paints, cleaning brushes and thinning – there may be special thinners to accompany some new products

Wax: beeswax, polish – if required, use instead of varnish on props to reduce reflection of light

Vaseline (*or motor oil*) – useful when making moulds and taking plaster casts

Brushes and rollers

Use sable brushes for painting scale models, hog's hair for general painting of props and larger bristle brushes for scenery. Wool or foam plastic rollers can also be used for scenery though brushes will still be required for detail.

For glue, use 18 mm or 25 mm round pure bristle brushes.

Electric or gas stove

A heat source is required for the heating of water, some kinds of glue, etc.

UK SUPPLIERS

Try local community or civic centre and information offices for assistance with the hire of all kinds of equipment at reasonable charges. Look in the Yellow Pages for local suppliers.

Art materials
paints, sable brushes, charcoal, P.V.A. adhesives

Atlantis Art Materials Ltd.
7/9 Plummer's Row
London E1 1EQ
Tel: 020 7377 8855

Daler-Rowney Ltd.
12 Percy Street
London W1A 2BP
Tel: 020 7636 8241

Dyes
Dylon, Procain

Dylon International Ltd.
Worsley Bridge Road
Lower Sydenham
London SE26 5HD
Tel: 020 8663 4801

Wood and hardboard
for flats and stage construction
All wood merchants (select *seasoned* softwoods if possible), hardware shops. Also try demolition contractors, junk yards, cheap secondhand furniture dealers, etc.

Cardboard and expanded polystyrene
Try electrical goods dealers, furniture and DIY shops for discarded cartons and packing.

Canvas
Brodie and Middleton Ltd
68 Drury Lane
London WC2B 5SP
Tel: 020 7836 3289

Scenic colour
pigments, aniline dyes, metallic powders and all sundries

Brodie and Middleton Ltd.
(address as before)

Stage draperies, flame-proof textiles, etc.
J. D. McDougall Ltd.
4 McGrath Road
Stratford
London E15 4JB
Tel: 020 8534 2921

Stage lighting and equipment
(also sound equipment, stage hardware)
Most lighting equipment illustrated in this book is manufactured by:

Strand Lighting Ltd.
Mitchelston Industrial Estate
Kirkcaldy
Fife KY1 3LY
Tel: 01592 652333
www.strandlighting.com

Strand Lighting's products are available through:

AJS Theatre Lighting & Stage Supplies Ltd.
Hightown Industrial Estate
Crow Arch Lane
Ringwood
Hampshire BH24 1ND
Tel: 01425 481100

Northern Light
39-41 Assembly Street
Leith
Edinburgh EH6 7RG
Tel: 0131 553 2383
www.northernlight.co.uk

Stage Electrics
Victoria Road
Avonmouth
Bristol BS11 9DB
Tel: 0117 938 4000
www.stage-electrics.co.uk

Make-up
Charles H. Fox Ltd
22 Tavistock Street
London WC2E 7PY
Tel: 020 7240 3111

Screenface
24 Powis Terrace
London W11 1JH
Tel: 020 7221 8289

Costume Hire
Academy Costumes Ltd.
50 Rushworth Street
London SE1 0RB
Tel: 020 7620 0771

Cosprop Ltd.
26-28 Rochester Place
London NW1 9JR

Royal Shakespeare Company
(Costume Hire Dept)
Timothys Bridge Road
Stratford-Upon-Avon
Warwickshire CV37 9UY
Tel/Fax: 01789 205920

Tools and adhesives
Local ironmongers and hardware shops

Paints and thinners
Local suppliers

US SUPPLIERS

Art supplies
Charrette
31 Olympia Avenue
Woburn, MA. 01888-4010
1-800-367-3729
www.charrette.com

Dick Blick
P.O. Box 1267
Galesburg, IL. 61401
1-800-447-8192
www.dickblick.com

Johnson's Artists' Supplies
355 Newbury Street
Boston, MA. 02115
(617) 536-4065

Costume rental
Norcostco
locations nationwide
www.norcostco.com

Chicago Costume Co. Inc.
1120 West Fullerton Street
Chicago, IL. 60614
(773) 528-1264
www.chicagocostume.com

Tracy Theatre Originals
70 High Street
Hampton, NH. 03842
(603) 926-8315
www.tracytheatreoriginals.com

Dyes
Dharma Trading Company
P.O.Box 150916
San Rafael, CA 94915
(800) 542-5227 (USA and Canada)
www.dharmatrading.com

Stage lighting and equipment
High Output
8 Diane Drive
Colchester, VT. 05446

Scenic material
Dudley Theatricals
3401 Indiana Avenue
Winston-Salem, NC. 27105
(336) 722-3255

Stage curtains and draperies
S & K Theatrical Draperies
7313 Varna Avenue
North Hollywood, CA. 91605
(800) 888-9177
(818) 503-0596

Rose Brand
75 Ninth Avenue, 4th Floor
New York, NY. 10011
(800) 223-1624
(212) 242-7554

10856 Vanowen Street
North Hollywood, CA. 91605
(800) 360-5056
(818) 505-6290

Make-up
Mehron
100 Red Schoolhouse Road
Chestnut Ridge, NY. 10977
(800) 332-9955

Ben Nye Company
5935 Bowcroft Street
Los Angeles, CA 90016
(310) 839-1984

INDEX

GENERAL INFORMATION

Fire precautions
Always contact your local fire service for all information and for a licence to perform.

Fireproofing solution
To make up a simple fireproofing solution mix the ingredients below:

Borax 10oz/285g
Boracic 8oz/227g
Tepid Water 1 gallon/4$\frac{1}{2}$l

or

Boracic Acid 15oz/425g
Sodium Phosphate 10oz/285g
Tepid Water 1 gallon/4$\frac{1}{2}$l

These are very crude mixtures and are for use cold. They will undoubtedly change the feel of the cloth. A dipped fabric should be hung up to dry and not wrung out. There are also products available from staging suppliers which work effectively when sprayed on light fabrics and are water resistant when dry.

Sound effects
Many traditional methods of making sounds have been superseded by the use of sound recordings. The use of coconuts for hooves, peas in a tray for rain, etc. are still useful but many typical sounds can now be obtained on a single CD. Look up lists of EMI and BBC publications. The thunder sheet (a large sheet of metal suspended in and above the wings) is still a useful sound effect. Music can be used for musicals etc. only if copyright is available. Advice/permission can be obtained from the Performing Rights Society which can be contacted at 29-33 Berners Street, London W1P 4AA.